iGNATiUS OF LOYOLA

To my VERY DEAR BROTHER in PRIESTHOOD
Father J. SENESPLADA, S.J.
in gratitude for your kindness to Poles
                                      from
        Fr. Balestar SZUBERLAK
        75% "JESUIT" educated
        in "GREGORIANUM"

EDINBURGH, 18-th of MAY, 1979. –

IGNATIUS OF LOYOLA

Karl Rahner SJ

with an Historical Introduction by Paul Imhof SJ

Colour Photographs by Helmuth Nils Loose

Translated by Rosaleen Ockenden

Collins

Published by Collins
London   Glasgow
Cleveland   New York   Toronto
Sydney   Auckland   Johannesburg

Original edition published in Germany as *Ignatius von Loyola*
© Verlag Herder, Freiburg im Breisgau 1978

First published in Great Britain 1979
UK ISBN 0 00 216346 2

First published in the USA 1979
Library of Congress Catalog Card Number 78-64484
USA ISBN 0-529-05643-7

Imprimi potest.
Monachii, dei 1.11.1977
P. Vitus Seibel SJ
Praep. Prov. Germ. Sup. SJ

Colour photographs by Helmuth Nils Loose
Engravings taken from the 1609 biography of Loyola

Made and printed by
Freiburger Graphische Betriebe 1978

Contents

Preface

It was an altogether praiseworthy plan to produce an illustrated volume about Ignatius of Loyola, as he is one of those great figures of the Church whose influence is still felt by us today. However, I felt there were only two people I knew ideally suited for writing an introductory text, since both were outstanding authorities on the subject of Ignatius of Loyola: my brother Hugo Rahner and my friend Burkhart Schneider. But my brother died in 1968 and my friend in 1976. Thus the task of writing the introductory text fell upon me. Out of friendship to the two of them I did not wish to refuse the offer, even though I am no historian and am far from being an expert on the history of the Jesuit Order or its founder.

I feel that I owe the reader an explanation about my introduction: I felt strongly that something needed to be written about what Ignatius means today. What I say, or rather put into the mouth of Ignatius, is naturally not an official opinion of any sort, nor an official programme for the Order today, but merely my own private subjective view which I put forward, fully conscious that it is subjectively selective and does not say all that there is to say nor even all that I would wish to say. If I make Ignatius speak for himself, the reader should not therefore judge what he says by literary standards; he ought not even to read into it subjective confessions on my part. My task was only to set out my opinion on the importance of Ignatius for our time. Since there were only these few pages at my disposal, I could not first portray Ignatius, his example and his teaching, in an historical context as objectively as possible and only then try to transpose him into our own time. There was simply no space. I had to portray the 'transposed' Ignatius from the beginning, in the hope that the transposition would sound right at least to some degree, and that it would strike the reader as convincing, precisely because such a transposition acts to a certain extent as a criterion for judging our own time and so must necessarily pass over a good deal that an historian as such would need to recount. For this reason it seemed to me easiest to let Ignatius speak for himself, as I have done here. I hope the reader will understand this and not suspect any further mysteries behind this method of presentation.

The second part of the text, the short biography of Ignatius, needs no extra introduction. It has been written by my colleague and brother in the Order, Paul Imhof SJ, who also prepared the text accompanying the illustrations.

Karl Rahner SJ   Munich, February 1978   7

Ignatius of Loyola
Speaks to a Modern Jesuit

I, Igna... ...a, intend to set down here, as best I can, some account of myself ... which faces Jesuits today, when (indeed because) they still feel the... ...l by the spirit that once inspired me and my first companions to foun... ...I do not propose to recount the story of my life in the manner ... ...al biography as I have already left you just such a brief report, w... ...v it towards the end of my life, and there have been quite enough ... ...od and bad, written about me in every century up to the present d... ...od's silence I will try to tell you something of myself, although ... ...s of the near impossibility of the task. Words that come from here ... ...again from eternity into time, even if this time remains shrouded i... ...al mystery. But do not say too quickly and easily that what I tell y... ...nged and made your own, since to be truly heard it has to touch *you*... ...rhaps *your* heart too and embrace all the questionable idiosyncrasi... ...her in his transitory situation. As a theologian you are well aware t... ...need not necessarily and totally deaden what is told. Even when y... ...en down what you yourself have heard, perhaps there will, nonethel... ...hing left in it of what I meant to say. And moreover: If what I have ... ...o sound exactly like my words in my account of my pilgrimage, in... ...es, in the Constitutions of my Order and in the thousands of l... ...I wrote together with my secretary Polance, if it could all be acc... ...lief as the mellow wisdom of a saint, then I would have spoken for ... ...and not for yours.

The D... ...rience of God

As you kn... ...desire was to 'help souls', as I put it in my day; to tell people about ... ...grace and about Jesus Christ, the Crucified and Risen, so that thei... ...ould become the freedom of God. I wanted to bring the same me... ...Church had always brought and yet I felt, and with reason, that I ... ...old message in new words. Why was this so? I was convinced that ... ...ively, during my illness in Loyola and then, decisively, during m... ...rmit in Manresa I had a direct encounter with God. This was the ex... ...ged to communicate to others.

When I claim to have known God at first hand, I do not intend here to add to my assertion a theological treatise on the nature of such a direct experience of God, nor a catalogue of all the accompanying phenomena of such an experience, which naturally have their own characteristics both personal and historical; I am not going to talk of forms and visions, symbols, voices, tears and such things. All I say is I knew God, nameless and unfathomable, silent and yet near, bestowing himself upon me in his Trinity, I knew God beyond all concrete imaginings. I knew Him clearly in such nearness and grace as is impossible to confound or mistake.

Such a conviction may sound quite harmless in your pious activities for which you prefer far more elevated language, yet fundamentally it is a monstrous claim from where I am now, able to experience quite differently how inconceivable God is, as well as from the viewpoint of the godlessness of your own time. In the end this lack of God simply eliminates the idols which the previous era, harmlessly and yet terribly, raised to the same level as the ineffable God. Why should I not say what I feel: it is a godlessness that affected even the Church, if the Church is intended ultimately, in union with the Crucified One, to be the cause of the fall of these gods through its own history.

Were you really never shocked that I said in my report of my pilgrimage that my mystical experiences had given me such certainty of faith that it would remain unshaken even if there were no Holy Scripture? Surely I laid myself open to the charge of subjective mysticism and disregard of the Church? It was indeed no surprise to me that I was suspected of being one of the illuminati in Alcalá and Salamanca and elsewhere. I truly encountered God, the living and true God, who merits this name which supersedes all other names. Whether such an experience is mystical or not is irrelevant here; how it is at all possible to make such an experience comprehensible using human concepts is for your theologians to speculate. Why such direct contact in no way invalidates a relationship with Jesus and consequently with the Church is something I will deal with later. But first: I encountered God, I knew him. Even then I could distinguish God himself from the words, images, and limited individual experiences which in some way direct man towards God. My experience naturally had a history of its own. It began in a small and undramatic way; I related it and wrote about it in a manner that now seems touchingly child-like even to me and allows the true meaning to be seen only indirectly and from afar. But one thing is sure: after Manresa, from then on, I knew the inscrutable incomprehensibility of God ever more intensely, ever more purely. My friend, Nadal, had already formulated it in his more philosophical way.

God himself: I knew God himself, not simply human words describing him. I knew God and the freedom which is an integral part of him and which can only be known through him and not as the sum total of finite realities and calculations about them. I knew him, even if knowing him 'face to face', as I do now, is again something different (and yet the same). I have no theological lecture to give on this difference. I simply tell you that this is how it was; I would even say: if you were to let your scepticism about such an assertion, sharpened as it is by an underlying atheism, go to the very limit, not just in cleverly expressed theory but in the bitter practice of life too, then you also might have the same experience. For it is then that it happens that death (although biologically you still go on living) is experienced as a radical hope, justifying itself through and by itself alone, *or* as absolute despair; and in this moment God offers himself. (It is not surprising that I was near the abyss of suicide that time in Manresa.) This experience is grace indeed and basically there is no one to whom it is refused. Of this I was sure and convinced.

The Prelude to my own Experience

The grace of Manresa was not something, either then or during the rest of my life, right up to the loneliness of my solitary death, that I considered as a special privilege granted to a chosen person, one of an elite. So I gave the Exercises to anyone to whom such an offer of spiritual help might seem acceptable. I handed out the Exercises even before I had studied your theology, before I had, not without some pains (I speak ironically), taken my doctorate in Paris, even before I had received ecclesiastical and sacramental authority through ordination. And why not? The master of the Exercises (as you came to call him later) in no way officially imparts the word of the Church as such, in spite of the spirituality of the Exercises, but rather provides, if he can, quite cautiously and from a distance, an opportunity for God and man to meet together truly and directly. My first companions were differently endowed in this respect and, before Paris, all those whom I had wanted to win over to my plans through the Exercises took to their heels and ran away. I ask again: Is this something so readily accepted both by the spirituality of my age and the atheism of yours, is it so much a matter of fact that the old era did not reject it as non-ecclesiastical subjectivity and your new era does not damn it as illusion and ideology?

In Paris I added the regulations of the ecclesiastical mind to my Exercises; I fought successfully through all the official ecclesiastical proceedings with which they encumbered me again and again, I placed my work and that of my companions under the direct guidance of the Pope. Of this I will give a more detailed account later. But one thing remains certain: God can and will come directly to man whom he has created; man, his creature, will know him truly when this happens; he will be aware of the sovereign power of God's freedom in his life, a freedom which cannot be computed (neither philosophically, nor theologically, nor 'existentially', nor dictated by human intelligence from appropriate arguments.

Ignatian Spirituality

This very simple and yet in reality stupendous conviction, together with something I have still to discuss, seems to me to be the core of what you today usually term my spirituality. Is it seen as part of the history of piety in the Church and is it new or old, natural or shocking? Does it mark the beginning of the Church's 'new era' and is it perhaps closer to Luther's and Descartes' original experiences than you Jesuits have wanted to admit to yourselves through the centuries? Is it something that will recede in our Church of today and tomorrow, in which people find the silent solitariness of God almost too much to bear and try to take refuge in Church community feeling, although this is something which ought to be built up from men who are spiritual and who have had direct contact with God and not from those who use the Church to avoid having anything to do with God and his free incomprehensibility. My friend, these questions are no longer questions for me and they need no answer from me; I am not here as a prophet of future Church history; but you must ask yourselves this question and find an answer that accords with theological clarity and the verdict of history.

One thing remains certain: it is possible for man to know God. And your cure of souls must keep this goal in mind, always, at every step, unwaveringly. If you fill up the barns of man's consciousness only with your very learned and up-to-date theology, which ultimately engenders nothing but a fearful torrent of words, if you were to train men only for piety, as zealous subjects of the ecclesiastical establishment, if you were to make the people in the Church no more than obedient subjects of a distant God, represented by an ecclesiastical hierarchy, if you were not to help men through all these difficulties, if you were not to help them finally to abandon all tangible assurances and isolated insights and go with confidence towards the inconceivable, where there are no longer paths and to achieve this at the final fearful ineluctable end of life and in the immeasurableness of love and joy and then, radically and ultimately, in death (with the dying Christ, abandoned by God), if you were not to help thus, then you would have either forgotten or betrayed my 'spirituality' in your so-called cure of souls and missionary task.

Perhaps because all men are short-sighted sinners, there have been many of you in the history of the Jesuits who have sinned through such forgetfulness and betrayal. You have not infrequently defended the Church as if she herself were the ultimate, as if she were not finally, if she is true to her own nature, the phenomenon in which man silently surrenders himself to God and in the final analysis no longer even wants to know what he is doing because God is an incomprehensible mystery and only as such can be our goal and our eternal happiness.

I should now explain more clearly, for you repressed secret atheists of today, how it is possible to meet God directly, until the time when this experience develops and God will meet man in everything and not only at special 'mystical' moments. Then everything will become clear and lead to God; I should in fact, mention the situations which are particularly favourable for such experiences (if these experiences are to be made clear for the first time). In your time such situations would not necessarily look exactly as I tried to envisage them in the advice accompanying my Exercises, even though I am convinced that these

Exercises can be yet more successful in your day, used fairly literally, than any fashionable 'improvements' on them which you may occasionally find cultivated today. I ought to have made it clearer that the dawn of such divine experience is not the indoctrination of something not previously present in man, but a more explicit awakening of and to the self, and the free acceptance of man's state of mind which is always a given factor, usually blocked and repressed, but inevitable; this is the grace in which God himself dwells in all his immediacy.

Perhaps, oddly enough, I should tell you that you have no reason to run like desperate men dying of thirst to Eastern sources of meditation, as if we ourselves no longer had sources of the living water. Nor should you, however, make the arrogant assertion that only human wisdom from the unconscious could flow from those sources and not genuine grace. But for now I have no more to say about these things. You yourselves must reflect on them, must search and put to the test. The true prize for this experience is the heart that gives itself in faith and hope and neighbourly love.

The Religious Institution and Inner Experience

I should like to put what I mean more clearly in a metaphor. Imagine man's heart as earth or soil. Is it to be damned to eternal unfruitfulness, to be a wilderness inhabited by demons, or is it to be a fertile land which brings forth the fruits of eternity? The Church, it may appear to an observer, sets up vast and complicated irrigation systems to bring water to the land of man's heart and to make it fruitful through her word, her sacraments, her institutions and practices. All such irrigation systems, if one may call them this, are certainly good and necessary (even if the Church itself admits that the soil of such a heart can bring forth eternal fruits even when it is not reached by the irrigation systems of the Church). Naturally this image may easily be misunderstood. Of course the Church's activity in preaching the gospel and administering the sacraments has aspects, bases and essentials which are not made plainer by this image.

Nonetheless, let us keep the image. In addition to these waters coming from without, led in, as it were, from the outside, which are intended to soak the land of the soul (without the image: in addition to the religious indoctrination, over and above God's principles and commandments, over and above everything which points only to God, including Church, Bible, sacraments and so on) there is also, so to speak, a well sited in the middle of this very land and from this source, once it has been bored, the waters of the living spirit gush forth into eternal life, as it is described in St John's Gospel. As has already been said, the image is askew; there is no ultimate contradiction between its own source and the eternal 'irrigation system'. Of course in real life these two aspects affect one another. To use another image: any appeal from outside in God's name is only an attempt to clarify God's inner promise of himself and this needs such an appeal in some earthly form, although the form may be more diverse and more unassuming than your theologians recognized earlier. Such an appeal from outside, an appeal of responsibility, of love and loyalty; of a selfless commitment to freedom and justice in society, may also sound far more worldly than your theologians would like to hear.

But I repeat yet again with dogged persistence: such indoctrinations and such imperatives from without, such channelling of grace from without, are ultimately only of use if they meet the final grace from within. This was my own actual experience ever since my very first 'Exercises' in Manresa, where the scales were lifted from my spiritual eyes and everything could be seen in God himself. This was the experience I longed to communicate to others through the Exercises I offered them.

It seems self-evident to me that it is more vital today than ever before to have such help towards a direct encounter with God (or should one say: towards an understanding of the fact that man has already come to meet God and truly meets him?), because otherwise there is an insuperable danger that all theological indoctrinations and all moral imperatives from without may be swallowed up in the deathly silence with which modern atheism surrounds the individual, obscuring the realization that this silence in fact still speaks of God. Still, again and again, I repeat: now I can no longer give my Exercises and so my assurance that man can meet God directly remains, of course, an unhonoured promise.

Do you understand now when I say that for you Jesuits the main task, around which everything else is focused, must be the giving of the Exercises. I in no way mean, of course, the official organization through the Church of courses which would be given to innumerable people at the same time, but rather a mystagogical help for others, so that they do not reject the immediate nearness of God but learn to know and accept it. Not that every one of you can or should give Exercises in this sense; you should not flatter yourselves that this is something you can do easily. Nor is this in any way a deprecation of all the other pastoral, academic, social and political activities which you have felt it necessary to attempt in the course of your history.

But you should understand all this as a preparation for or continuation of your ultimate task both now and in the future: to help others to experience God directly and to realize that the incomprehensible mystery that we call God is near and we can talk to him. It is precisely then that he harbours us safely, if we do not try to make him subject to us but rather surrender ourselves unconditionally to him. All you do should be tested to see if it serves this purpose. If it does, then one of you may, if he is a biologist, investigate the spiritual life of the cockroach if he will.

God's Love for the World

When I say that it is as possible to encounter God in your age as in mine, I mean God really and truly, the God of incomprehensibility, the ineffable mystery, the darkness which only becomes eternal light for the man who allows himself to be swallowed up by it unconditionally. But it is precisely this God, he and none other, whom I personally experienced as the God who comes down to us, who comes close to us, the God in whose incomprehensible fire we are not, in fact, burnt away but become ourselves and of eternal value. The ineffable God promises himself to us; and in this promise of his ineffability we become, we live, we are loved and we are of eternal value; through him, if we allow ourselves to be taken up by him, we are not destroyed but given to ourselves truly for the first time. The vain and idle creature becomes infinitely important, inexpressibly great and beautiful, because God himself endows it with himself.

Without God we would wander around eternally insecure and ultimately despairing and bored in the sphere of our freedom and of our decisions, because everything we might choose would be finally finite and ever replaceable by something else and would therefore remain indistinguishable. I made the discovery, however, that in the sphere of this my freedom and its possibilities the infinitely free God of all my possibilities enfolded one possibility rather than another with his especial love, let it shine through directly to him, so that it did not obscure him but made him loved in it and it in him and so showed itself as 'the will of God'.

When I put the possibilities for my freedom apprehensively and tentatively before the imminent decision of my freedom, then I discovered that one possibility, shining through into the open freedom, related to God himself and led openly to him and the other possibility did not, even though all such possibilities could in themselves be minute symbols of the eternal God, which all stem from him each in its own way. In this way more or less (it is difficult to explain clearly) I learned to distinguish within the field of the factually and rationally possible and the socially and ecclesiastically permitted, between something in which the inconceivable nature of the limitless God was near me in the midst of limitation and something, although experienced empirically and meaningful in itself, which remained, as it were, gloomy and impenetrable on the path towards God. It would therefore be simply foolish to say that everything that is real and true, just because it is real and comes from God, must lead every individual to him equally, because every inevitable decision of freedom would then be indistinguishable from every other.

God 'becomes flesh' in his creature and yet his creature does not falter the nearer he comes to God but, for the first time, feels his true worth: this is the experience, yet not all the experience. Incomprehensible as it may seem, God's descent into finiteness takes place through his creature who has attained his very presence. The nameless, incomprehensible, inflexible, incalculable God may not disappear from the sight of the man who prays and acts, God may not become like the sun which makes everything visible and is himself not seen. God must remain immediate and must, indeed, hold firm everything else in its finiteness and relativity with relentless clarity.

But the creature who is singled out from every other creature by the bestowal of God's love appears in this merciless light as the one beloved and preferred, as the one chosen for existence among many empty possibilities. The man who stands in God's eternal light takes part in God's unfolding towards the fixed and finite creature; he may and can take this finiteness with real seriousness, for him it is lovable, beautiful, of ultimate, eternal validity, because God himself can and does bring to fulfilment the inconceivable miracle of his love by giving himself to his creature. Faced with this realization of God's affection, of his descent into the finite without either being diminished himself or consuming the finite, man can no longer be someone whose most secret terror and desire is to lay bare the relativity and insignificance of everything and everyone. He can no longer be someone who either idolizes or (ultimately) destroys what is fixed and finite. The unfolding of God's affection for something that is not God and that through this affection, unalloyed, can no longer be separated from God is experienced first when something is felt to be willed by God in contrast to something else, as I have already explained. Since, however, this other to whom God shows himself is, in concrete and precise terms, the nearest man and not an object, God's movement towards man is realized in true love of man's neighbour. This is something I will return to later. The love for God, which seems to mean the decline of the world, is a love of the world which includes God in its love and so means not its decline but its eternal rising.

God's Coming into the World is Fulfilled

But these are only words about an experience and cannot conjure up the experience itself. The experience of God's act of fulfilment has to be made in real life. Here too, as so often in other spheres, the whole cannot be put together out of pieces previously rent asunder; it has to be bestowed as a whole and only then and thus can it develop in its unity and multiplicity and be made part unconditionally of man's freedom. Man's neighbour has to be loved with unsolicited mater-of-factness in everyday life, loved ever more selflessly and honestly. God must manifest himself more and more plainly in his absoluteness. Love of God and love of man's neighbour must impress themselves ever more clearly on man's freedom in their insoluble unity, in their mutually conditional relationship.

Love of his neighbour presents itself initially as the more natural course to the man who has gone out into the vanity of the world. Yet at the same time this love is always in danger of dying in desperation and disappointment at the emptiness of the lover and of the beloved. So today as always we have to begin determined to do what is not automatic, to seek God as a direct presence, to carry out the Exercises in this sense (which has above all nothing to do with Exercise houses, officially organized Church courses, detailed theological indoctrination, etc.). At all events, love of God (of God himself, and not of a human theory about him!) is the ultimate reason for a love of man's neighbour that can be unconditional and yet remain free.

Christian meditation as a way of experiencing the immediacy of God does not cause the world to recede and disintegrate. In the case of the Eastern meditations that are considered so fascinating today, as if nothing of equal value could be found inside Christianity, you must test for yourselves whether the same is true. If it is so, then I must concur in your fondness for the East and see God at work here too, pouring out his spirit over all flesh; if not, then you would do well to be cautious.

In any case you ought not to mean to succumb today to the temptation that, in order to be itself, the silent and infinite incomprehensibility which we call God could or might not turn towards you in free love, not come to meet you, not empower you from your innermost heart where it dwells to say 'Thou' with confidence to this Nameless One. This incomprehensible miracle which breaks the bounds of all your metaphysics, whose potential is only realized when its reality is tested, is a miracle which itself is part of the ineffability of God. It would remain an empty formality still subject to your metaphysics, if and when it were not experienced as part of God's affection for us. You must be on your guard today as always against thinking that this familiarity is the preliminary step to the fall into God's silent incomprehensibility; it is rather a consequence of that fall, it blossoms as the fulfilment of surrender to God's affection for us, it allows God to be greater than we think him, if only we understand ourselves as unceasingly dependent and worthless.

Jesus

Now I must speak of Jesus. Perhaps it seemed, in all that I have said up until now, as if I had forgotten Jesus and his blessed Name? No so, for he was present implicitly in all I have said, even though my words necessarily come one after the other and so cannot convey all I mean simultaneously. When I say 'Jesus', you will say in your 'history of devotion' that the devotion to Jesus that I seek to foster in the Exercises is only a continuation and echo of that devotion to Jesus which was common throughout the Middle Ages from Bernard of Clairvaux until Francis of Assisi and after. You will say that at most I added on a few concepts drawn from late medieval feudalism, although that was already on the wane in the secular world.

I willingly admit that you can discover many such traits of medieval piety centred on Jesus in my writings. I dispense you today willingly from looking back to the Mount of Olives to see exactly what happened with the footprints that the Lord left behind when he ascended into heaven. Why indeed should I take it to heart if I am accused of lacking originality in this matter? Is this medieval devotion to Jesus obsolete or does it contain a message that is not understood today? It surely contains a promise to provide what your modern devotion to Jesus is looking for. You claim only to find man truly when you pompously and naively proclaim the death of God instead of realizing that it is in man that God has expressed himself and promised himself.

In my day it was no problem for me to find God in Jesus and Jesus in God – or, at most, a problem of love and true discipleship. I could find God in him in an unique way, in a truly factual sense, so that love alone and not discriminating reason can say how he should be imitated by a disciple. The history of God, eternal and incomprehensible, can be told and has been told about him. It must be told anew again and again and so continue its own story. For me, since my conversion, Jesus was the epitome of God's love of the world and of me, the love in which the incomprehensibility of the pure mystery is implicit and in which man comes to his own fullness. I was never perturbed by the uniqueness of Jesus, by the necessity of searching him out in a limited store of facts and words, of trying to find in this smallness the infinity of the ineffable mystery. The journey to the Holy Land was for me truly a journey into the pathlessness of God and it is you, not I, who are simplistic and superficial to imagine that my fifteen years of yearning for the Holy Land was merely the whim of a medieval man or much the same as a modern Muslim's desire to see Mecca. My desire for the Holy Land was a longing for Jesus, the concrete Jesus and no abstract idea.

The Christianity which can bypass Jesus to find the incomprehensible God does not exist. God has willed that many, unutterably many, should find Jesus simply because they *seek* him. When they die, they die with Jesus who was abandoned by God, even if they do not know this blessed name to describe their fate. God has only let this darkness of finiteness and guilt into his world, because in Jesus he made them also his own.

It was this Jesus that I loved, this Jesus I sought to follow. And for me all this was the way in which I truly found God without making him merely into the figment of my untrammelled speculation. For it is only possible to rise above such speculation by travelling through life and dying a true death. To die this death well, that abandonment by God which is part of death and also the ultimate mysticism has to be calmly accepted in company with Jesus. I know that in saying this I am far from explaining the mystery of the unity of history and God. But in the Crucified and Risen Jesus, that is, in his leaving of God and his receiving of God, this unity is ultimately present and can be accepted in faith, hope and love.

To Be a Disciple of Christ

I have more to say about this Jesus and about following him as his disciple, imitating him lovingly, even foolishly. I claim no originality for it, since here too it is the old message coming to you from a future you have not as yet reached. Jesus is truly found and God found in him only when you have died with him. But when it is understood that this dying with Jesus must happen through life, then certain individual aspects of Jesus' life take on a frightening significance in spite of their apparent fortuitousness and their historical and social conditioning. I do not know whether these individual aspects of the ordinary life of Jesus, which came to rule my life, are of clear and especially cogent importance for all men who, explicitly or anonymously, find God and are saved. It seems not to be so.

There seem to be many ways of being a follower of Jesus. There is no real point in reducing all these ways to one common denominator, in distilling one unified essence of discipleship from the many concrete forms of such discipleship by saying that 'in spirit' they are all one and the same. That may be very true; there is naturally a single ultimate essence of discipleship, because there is one God, one Jesus, one man more or less the same and one same eternal life. But there are concrete forms of this discipleship which are different, which remain terribly different, which even seem to threaten or contradict one another.

Innocent III and Francis of Assisi did not practice the same discipleship, for instance. These two forms of discipleship were so different (and yet neither was challenged as a way of following Christ) that they could only just tolerate developing side by side with one another in almost desperate love and patience. There are surely many different charisms and perhaps no one can truly comprehend more than one of them, the charisma that he himself possesses.

However that may be, I chose the discipleship of the poor and humble Jesus and no other. Such a choice has the total illogicality of true love, it is a vocation which carried its own legitimization within it. It is far from being simply something which should be enjoined upon all Christians or could be enjoined upon them all with the trick explanation that it is a question of poverty and humility in spirit and attitude. I make no claim to originality here and saints in heaven do not compare themselves with one another, but apart perhaps from the outward style of my life in my last years as General of the Order, I practised poverty in my life after Manresa just as radically as Francis of Assisi. Naturally it has to be taken into account that the times in which we lived were socially and economically very different and so there were necessarily differences in our lifestyles too. In particular, in contrast to Francis, I both wanted and had to study – the consequent differences even a St Bonaventura himself would have observed and approved without disputing that I too was truly a disciple of the Jesus of poverty. If you would only read my account of my pilgrimage you would understand what I mean.

As a result of this discipleship of the Jesus of humility, moreover, I found that there arose a spiritual and ecclesiastical way of life from the situation which existed then, which was not only irreconcilable with *secular* positions of power, but also excluded *ecclesiastical* power, ecclesiastical benefices and episcopal honours. I was totally serious about my decision to remain on the fringe (if I may call it that) both in secular and ecclesiastical society. It was in no way something that was forced on me from outside.

I was born into one of the best Basque families and was connected with the great men of the world and the Church of my time. It would have been easy for me to become somebody. I could even have had the reassuring consciousness that in doing so I was serving my fellow-men, the Church and God unselfishly and self-sacrificingly through my power and rank. I could even perhaps have said to myself, without self-deception, that I could achieve better things from such a social position in Church and world than if I became an insignificant poor wretch on the edge of society and the Church. (The fact that I became a quite different person again through the founding of my Order and my position as General of it is something of which I have yet to speak.)

In short, I wanted to follow the poor and humble Jesus and no other. I wanted something that does not come of itself, which cannot be derived from 'the essence of Christianity', something which the prelates of the Church and the higher clergy in the countries which still regard themselves as bulwarks of Christianity did not practise then and do not now. I wanted something that was not determined for me by the ideology of the Church nor by social criticism, even though both played some part. I wanted something that my foolish love of Jesus Christ inspired in me as the law of my life, with no deviation to left or right. Without its total factualness—in spite of its finite and conditional nature—I could not find the eternal and incomprehensible God. I include rather than exclude the fact that being on the fringe of society and the Church was for me a free practice, as it were, for dying with Jesus. This is the judgement and happy fate for all men, even for those who cannot or will not follow Jesus in this way.

Service without Power

How hard I strove (and how successfully!) during my time on earth to prevent my people being promoted to episcopal and similar posts. Not because I did not want the best people to be taken away from my small flock. If a Jesuit becomes a bishop or a cardinal today you see nothing odd in it, it would seem to you to be basically quite normal that there should be and indeed were, times when a Jesuit cardinal was almost a permanent fixture in the Curia.

Can you not see how different your mentality and mine are here? You will say that times were different then. Today you no longer become a powerful lord through such an appointment. But it is not true! Firstly cardinals and bishops even today are people who are considerably beset by the temptation of power. And secondly you would have to ask yourselves, if you were right, where the positions, offices, controls and so on are in the Church today, which you would have to refuse resolutely in the same spirit as I did, in order to serve mankind through the Church trusting purely and simply in the power of the spirit and the folly of Christ.

You may indeed with a quiet mind become a bishop like Helder Camara who risks life and limb for the poor. But consider where the 'episcopal chairs' are today, perhaps under a different name, which you should not occupy, even though it can be shown that they are indispensable to the Church. I know the fundamental problem here: how can a charismatic society of radical discipleship of Jesus also be an ecclesiastically institutionalized order? Naturally I was pleased to have the Pope's official approval of the Order even during my life-time. And you have to try constantly to achieve the miracle of uniting the two. The sum will never work out exactly. But keep trying! One of the two on its own is too little. Only when the two are multiplied is it enough.

When I speak of the 'poor' and 'humble' Jesus whose disciple I wanted to be, then you today have to translate these words into theory and practice so that you really understand them. You have to ask yourselves what 'poor and humble' actually means *today*, in your time? If one becomes a Jesuit today, one becomes, perhaps quite quickly and automatically, a good man and a good priest. But not poor and humble, not by a long way. How this practical translation into the reality of modern life ought to look is something you will have to work out for yourselves. Perhaps some of you have to discover it for yourselves, before it can become clear in the Order as a whole. But for God's sake do not take refuge in a state of mind shared by the prelates of the Church. Poverty and humility in today's terms must have social and political implications in secular society and in the Church; they must also have a critical sting, a dangerous memory of

Jesus and provide a threat to the automatic activity of Church institutions. Otherwise your translation is worthless. This is merely a criterion for you, however, not a true motive: the motive is Jesus, dying unto death, Jesus himself and not a socio-political calculation. He alone can preserve you from the fascination of power which exists in a thousand forms in the Church and which will always remain there; he alone can rescue you from the only too plausible thought that basically you can only serve mankind by having power; he alone can make the Holy Cross of his powerlessness understandable and acceptable.

Successful and Unsuccessful Discipleship

I am not, however, to be spared from saying something about the fate of my life-style in the discipleship of the poor and humble Jesus and the fate that this life-style has had on my Order. If one looks at this history from the viewpoint of Divine Eternity, enfolded by the loving Will of God without which there would be nothing that really was and is, then one sees such a history calmly and collectedly with its own personal meaning and its own truth. There is then no dilemma about whether to take such history simply as personal history or whether to condemn it as the sons' apostasy from the father's spirit. In spite of this proviso, which you must bear in mind, I have to tell you Jesuits that in this respect, at any rate up to the present time, my Order has not followed me.

Of course there have been poor and humble people among you in real life and not just in theory. Peter Claver, for instance, the slave of slaves in Latin America, Franz Regis who shared the fate of his poor peasants, Friedrich von Spee who stood by the witches in danger of his life and of exclusion from the Order, the many Jesuits who in earlier centuries voyaged in indescribable ships to East Asia merely, in fact, in order to be slaughtered there, and many many others right down to your friend Alfred Delp, who signed his vow to the Order with bound hands before he was hanged in Berlin in 1945: all these were without a doubt true followers of the poor and humble Jesus and inspired by the same spirit that I have handed down to you through the Order. But what of the Order as such, apart from these individuals?

You know how I prayed and wrestled for weeks over apparent details of the vow of poverty in my Order in order to protect the spirit of Jesus, poor and humble, through rules. Yet these were details which you would probably have settled in a few hours of sober and rational discussion. You know that viewed as a whole, soberly and honestly, I did not succeed through my laws, just as Francis did not succeed (I ask pardon of the Franciscans) in preserving real discipleship of the really poor Jesus for the Order as such.

Perhaps, in fact *such* a spirit cannot be defended by laws because they either kill the spirit that they want to defend or inevitably leave so much freedom that another spirit can fill the space without offending the letter of the law. Perhaps the proposed life-style cannot suit a larger group without substantial alterations being made. Perhaps I had already crossed the decisive boundary with my companions, all inspired by the same spirit as I, when in 1540 we changed this 'charismatic' circle (as you would call it today) into an ecclesiastically approved Order. But ought we not to have done this, when it was in fact the means by which the last impulses of God's spirit continued to take effect for centuries to come?

It is possible too that a calm and humble renunciation of the purity and unfetteredness of the 'ideal' is also part of the spirit which alone truly brings the history of the Church and the world nearer to God. It is perhaps not surprising in this world, in which the spirit has to find physical expression in society—a process which threatens to kill it—that the Order has become a place of economic security and, at the very least, ecclesiastical prestige for its members, even if the individual within it lives modestly in economic terms and only rarely does one of them (more rarely than in comparable circumstances) become a bishop or a cardinal or otherwise powerful in the Church. Should this be regarded as a foregone conclusion or is it a tragedy?

Is it necessary anyway that what was a moral obligation in the past should hold good for Jesuits in the future? There is the possibility that, whether they wish it or not, Jesuits might in the future become economically poor as an Order in a very real sense, live hand to mouth as the genuinely poor do and accept this willingly and without faltering in union with the Jesus of poverty. This could then, as a consequence and not as a reason, have importance as social criticism. It is also possible that the Jesuits, for reasons I cannot foresee, might suddenly again be forced onto the fringe in a completely new and different way in Church society and adopt a healthy charismatic distance to the hierarchy, while naturally continuing to respect it. Recently J. B. Metz has made some thought-provoking comments on this subject. Such considerations present questions which are answered in the eternity where I am, but the answers are only transposed into your time by history and not by hasty words.

At any rate you Jesuits have the duty of courage in the face of the future, because Jesus in his actual life and death presents us with a legitimate life-style for the future too. Only you have to find out for yourself what this life-style should be tomorrow in order to be a true disciple of the poor and humble Jesus. I have talked about Jesus as 'poor' and 'humble' in the idiom of my own time. I should again emphasize that you will perhaps have to translate these words into different terms, so that you can understand them and live them without taking refuge in mere opinions or in a purely private and self-profiting asceticism, as has been your tendency during the last century and a half. Throughout that time you have not seen clearly enough your social responsibility for justice in the world, nor has the Church as a whole in spite of some praiseworthy encyclicals.

Devotion to the Church

I must also say something about my devotion to the Church and its importance for your time.

Everyone expects me to do so and quite rightly. If it were a question of assessing objectively the importance of the subjects I am discussing in all their variety, then I would have to let a few words suffice. If God, Jesus, his discipleship and the Church are all to be differentiated from one another, in spite of being closely connected, and therefore given different weight, then I have not only the right but also the duty in time and eternity to distinguish between the significance and importance of these various realities. Great stress is put upon the fact that I am a man of the Church; Marcuse calls me a soldier of the Church.

In truth I am not ashamed of this attachment to the Church. I wanted to serve the Church with my whole life after my conversion, even if ultimately this service was for God and man and not for a self-seeking institution. The Church has infinite dimensions because it is a community of people, pilgrims who believe and hope, who love God and their neighbour and are filled with God's spirit. But the Church is also, and for me quite naturally so, a socially constructed actual Church, an historical fact, a Church of institutions, of the human word, tangible sacraments, of bishops, of the Pope of Rome, it is the hierarchical Roman Catholic Church. And when I am called a man of the Church, and I readily admit to it, then it is precisely the Church in its tangible hard institutionalism that is meant, the official Church, as you term it today with the not altogether pleasant nuance that the word has. Yes, I was and wanted to be this man of this Church and never seriously found that there was any absolute conflict between it and the radical nearness of the God of my conscience and my mystical experience.

But my devotion to the Church is totally misunderstood, if it is understood as the egotistic, fanatically and ideologically restrictive love of power which triumphs over the conscience or as a form of identification with a 'system' which does not have any vision beyond itself. Since we men are all sinful and short-sighted during our lives, I will not try to maintain that I have not now and then in my lifetime paid tribute to this false attachment to the Church and you may, if you so will, search through my life soberly and honestly for traces of it. But one thing is sure: my devotion to the Church had in general only one imperative motive for me, which was my desire 'to help souls', a desire which only reaches its true goal when these 'souls' grow in faith, hope, love and nearness to God.

To love an official Church would be idolatry, participation in the terrible egoism of a system made for itself, if it were not inspired and limited by such a desire. This means, however, as the story of my mystical path proves, that my love for this Church, unconditional as it is in one sense, was far from being the be-all and end-all of my existence (as you say today), but a secondary force which springs from a nearness to God and receives from it its boundaries and its own distinctive mark.

To put this in another way: I loved the Church as the realization of God's love for the physical body of his son in history. In this mystical union of God with the Church—in spite of the radical difference between them—the Church itself was and remained a way to God for me and the point of my inexpressible relationship to the eternal mystery. Here lies the source of my views on the Church, of my practice of sacramental life, of my loyalty to the papacy and of the bond between the Church and my mission to help souls.

If my devotion to the Church has this place in the complex structure of my spiritual existence, this and no other, then a critical attitude to the actual official Church is in itself devout. Such a critical attitude on the part of the Christian is possible because his viewpoint is not necessarily identical with that of the official Church in its external institutional form. The Christian is also in direct contact with God and his inspiration (however much it leaves him as part of the Church and itself belongs to the Church as a community of grace) is not simply imparted through the ecclesiastical apparatus. It may be something from which the official Church and its representatives should learn, if they do not want to be guilty of rejecting these movements of the Spirit, which have already been officially approved by the Church.

Such a critical attitude towards the Church is, seen from her point of view, even devout in itself, since, because of God's dwelling in her, the Church as an institution remains ultimately open and subordinate to the Spirit, which is far greater than any institution, law, or literal tradition, etc. Of course, the existence of this relationship between spirit and institution does not eliminate actual conflicts between those Christians inspired by the spirit and the official representatives of the Church. Such conflicts recur in surprisingly new forms, so that there are no ready solutions and institutional mechanisms at hand to overcome them.

Finally, only in faith can a Christian be convinced that fundamentally and until the end of time there is no necessity for any absolute conflict between spirit and institution in the Church. For himself he can only hope in humility that God's providence will prevent any situation from arising for him personally in which an absolute decision of the official Church and an absolute decision of his conscience are no longer able to be reconciled. In any case partial and limited conflicts in the Church are even desirable, although I stop short of proposing actual plans for their implementation. Thus the literal execution of an order from above is not the highest injunction of devotion to the Church and ecclesiastical obedience and I myself as General of my Order have never governed by means of such an injunction. Indeed there would be no conflicts in the Church, if it were the highest injunction. It exists as an injunction, nonetheless, and rightly so, even in the case of the saints (beginning with the dispute between Peter and Paul).

There is no principle in the Church which says that the convictions and decisions of Christians and office-holders should automatically integrate without friction. The Church is a Church of the spirit of the infinite and incomprehensible God, whose perfect unity can only be mirrored in this world in many different facets. The Church's final perfected unity is God himself and nothing else.

So do not think that in my devotion to the Church I was spared the experience of such conflicts or that I managed to bypass them with a false devotion. I was no Janitshar of the Church and the Pope. I was in conflict with Church officials in Alcalá, Salamanca, Paris, Venice and Rome. I was locked up for weeks by the officials in Alcalá and Salamanca; in Rome too all the uproar when I defended my devotion to the Church cost me a terrible amount of time and effort. When the Eternal Father promised me in La Storta that he would keep me in mind in Rome, one of the possible forms which I imagined this 'favour' might take was a crucifixion in papal Rome. All the bones in my body shook when Paul IV was elected Pope. It was he who ordered his police to search my house even though I was already the General of an Order which had papal approval. I would have liked his blessing on my deathbed, in order to make an unassuming and courteous gesture towards him even at that hour, since I was dying without the sacraments; but when Polanco brought the blessing, I was already dead and the Pope's reaction on hearing the news was not exactly amiable.

In short, I was and remained devoted to both Church and Pope; but I was nonetheless harried and imprisoned by the Church's men acting on official authority. You will remember that in general the unity between obedient service and critical distance towards the ministry of the Church has always been accompanied by such conflicts. Yet the unity has been realized successfully even without there being any generally applicable rules valid once and for all. A very close look has to be taken at the history of the Order before devotion to Church and Pope can be seen as a subject of praise or blame. One saint, Pius V, meddled with the Order, showing no understanding at all of its true nature. In the so-called Dispute about Grace, the Order with its theology had to defend itself in Rome and only just managed to obstruct a verdict. The Order had to fight for its moral theology in the face of an alliance between Innocent XI and its own General of the Order, Gonzalez; in the seventeenth and eighteenth centuries you lost the dispute over rites with Popes who cared more for orthodox prudence than creative courage. The suppression of the Order in 1773 by Clement XIV (with the rather shabby text of the suppression brief and the unworthy incarceration of the General of the Order, Ricci, by the Pope, against whom Amnesty International would be mobilized today) was carried out under pressure from the Bourbons (who were shortly afterwards swept away by the Revolution and so would have easily been put off by a show of rather more resistance). It was certainly no heroic piece of papal wisdom and courage, however wisely and clearly it may be explained away by historians. Saint Pius X was intent upon deposing Wernz, the General of the Order, because he was not integralist enough.

There are many similar examples which might be cited of the critical distance which existed between the official Church and the Order. It would perhaps be better if it were possible to maintain that the Order's renunciation of any claim to the dignity of bishops and cardinals—in fact, a fundamental move to detach itself from the otherwise approved and respected offices in the Church—must have automatically caused the appearance of such conflicts. However the institutionalization of the connections between Order and office in other ways had in fact, partly frustrated the real sense of this move to abandon ecclesiastical honours.

This is not in any way to deny that in the course of the long history of my Order, the interests of the Order and the official ministry have often been identical at times when a critical distance and legitimate resistance would have been more appropriate. In fact, the Order had constantly incurred historic guilt by defending the ecclesiastical institution with its myopia and lethargic immobility in theology, pastoral care and law, instead of defending the spirit of the Church.

Fundamentally it remains a fact that unconditional loyalty to the institutional Church and a critical detachment towards her spiritually was a genuine possibility for me and my companions and that it has its part to play in the true nature of the Church.

So today you need not feel too disturbed because Paul VI was not entirely happy about your 32nd General Congregation. It was much more serious at the time of Pius V and Sixtus V, who both wanted to impose upon you sensitive alterations of your constitution. There are some among you today who are certainly odd figures and it is difficult to see why they still remain Jesuits. In general, however, your Jesuits are still loyal to Church and Pope as I was and this loyalty inevitably brings conflict with it.

The Obedience of the Jesuits

At this point it is perhaps opportune as an addition to the subject of devotion to the Church, to say something about so-called 'Jesuit obedience'. I make no claim to originality as regards the history of piety either, even though naturally enough obedience inevitably has greater importance in an active Order engaged on a common mission than it has in an abbey of contemplatives. And this is especially true when a world-wide Order is centrally administered and therefore the connections between its individual members cannot be regulated on the basis of acquaintance or friendship. Basically I hold the same views now as always on this subject both in theory and in practice. To have the intention of obedience, to have the determination to make yourself available for a common task involving many and to integrate and subordinate yourself in that community, all this is not an attitude of which to be ashamed, even today. Decisions that have to be taken for a community and which are binding on the individual cannot always be considered, discussed and even postponed until absolutely everyone has seen the practical correctness of a certain decision for himself. Such a 'democratic' process of decision-making may be all very well and indeed possible in small groups. It is, however, utopian to expect it to be possible always and everywhere that a decision is required.

In the case of such decisions, which are almost always decisions in questions of opinion either completely or partially, it is not easy to see why subordinating yourself to a decision you do not yourself consider to be the better should offend your sense of your own dignity. It is naturally a prerequisite that you should approve of the unity of the community and wish to work in a common cause, that you should have that equability and calm towards the various possibilities of life and action and that readiness to be self-critical and not self-important which is enjoined upon you in the fundamentals of the Exercises as the ruling principle of your spirituality.

I do not want to discuss here the question of obedience as part of the discipleship of Jesus. In my teaching on obedience I am in any case not so 'democratic' that I think a binding decision is always in every case more probably right and reasonable if it has been taken by a collective decision-making process instead of an individual, if in both cases the decision taken runs counter to the opinion of the person concerned. Both methods of arriving at a decision have their advantages and disadvantages. A collective verdict is not always clearer and it is often impossible to find anyone who can be considered responsible for it. In the secular world a 'democratic centralism' is far from completely outmoded, even today. In my Order too (in contrast to the constitution of the Church), the highest authority is a parliament elected from below, the General Congregation. The Superior General himself is responsible to it, even though he has very wide-ranging powers on the executive. Has it ever occurred to you that the constitutional principle of your Order is more democratic than that of the papacy governing the whole Church, for which you have entered the lists so vigorously in the course of your history? Have you ever reflected on the fact that to call the head of your Order 'the black Pope' is a misnomer in view of the democratic principles of your constitution?

All Jesuit obedience is, in addition, encompassed by a fraternal community, nonetheless genuine and effective for being sober and practical, and demanding of the individual the sacrifice of some of the warmth of the nest. Besides you could today de-mythologize the traditional teaching on obedience a little, despite the unconditional nature of rational obedience—even, perhaps, what I dictated to Polanco in my famous letter on obedience. It does not count as eternal truth. Today a 'subordinate' has fewer inhibitions about answering with a quiet but definite 'no' to an order given by a superior in good faith, if he simply cannot reconcile it with his conscience.

Even if you believe that God's providence is at work in the government of the Church and the Order, it is not necessary to think that 'superiors' have a more direct and sure telephonic communication, as it were, with heaven or that their decisions, in spite of being binding, are more than discretionary decisions taken in good faith, subject to reservations and possibilities of error in any individual case.

Anyone who is equable, self-critical and prepared to work quietly to serve a common cause, and who has in addition a touch of humour and easy understanding for the follies and vagaries of earthly history, has no especially difficult problems with obedience in an Order today. It seems to me even that a middle-class father of a family or civil servant would have a narrower range of freedom in secular society today than you have in an Order. In spite of the rash and stupid phrase in the Letter of Obedience, you do not need to practice a corpse-like obedience. But you must be selfless, sober and serviceable. There is a 'mysticism of service', which I will not speak of at the moment. This de-mythologizing is certainly also essential today with regard to 'obedience' to secular powers and the powers of the state. In the course of history you have far too often been devoted 'subjects' of secular authorities, although you had no need to be according to the theories of your great baroque theologians. Why, for instance did you not in the eighteenth century, together with your Indians, defend by force the holy experiment of the Reductions against the hideous colonialism of Europe? Did you really have to allow yourselves to be forced out of Latin America in the name of devout obedience?

Learning and Study in the Order

I am tempted to say something on the subject of the history of theology in my Order, even if very little can be adduced from it that is of value for the future of this theology. But I must content myself with a few small comments, even though the history itself is not without significance. The theory of probabilism which your moral theologians defended was a great affair for its time in the defence of the right of the individual to freedom of conscience, even if today it is necessary to express the idea in a quite different form.

The fact that you were humanists of a modern mentality in your theology and that you thought with a definitely modern optimism about 'natural' man, the fact that you drew conclusions from this about your missions in China and India which were not approved by Rome, all contributed, intentionally or otherwise, to the beginnings of a theological anthropology, such as there should be in a Church which aims to be the Church for the whole world and all cultures, and not just European Christianity as an export to the rest of the world. Your mistake in this optimistic kind of anthropology from below was in letting a large number of your theologians transfer divine grace into another world of the consciousness, contrary to the fundamental conviction of my Exercises. It was their opinion that without real experience it was only possible to know this grace through external indoctrination by the Church.

Just as your theology contributed with history and law to the development of the Church's understanding of faith, which was worked out at the First Vatican Council, so your theology today is equally under an obligation to develop further the advances in the Church's constitutional law which were made plain in Vatican II. You must remain loyal to the papacy in theology (and in practice), because that is part of your heritage to a special degree, but since the actual form of the papacy remains subject, in the future too, to an historical process of change, your theology and ecclesiastical law has above all to serve the papacy as it will be in the future, so that it will be a help and not a hindrance to the unity of Christendom. In addition, study Marx, Freud and Einstein, try to evolve a theology which can touch the ear and heart of men today. But the point of departure and the end of your theology, which even today should have the courage to be genuinely systematic, remains Jesus Christ, the Crucified and Risen Lord. He is the triumphant promise made by the comprehensible God to his world. He and not some spiritual fashion or other which is here today and gone tomorrow is your beginning and your end.

Your theology has often been reproached with a cheap eclecticism and there is some truth in the slur. But if God is the 'ever greater God' who breaks the bounds of every system which man uses to try to make reality subject to him, then your 'eclecticism' can be the expression of the fact that man is over-taxed by God's truth and accepts this system in which you can comprehend the whole of reality from the one point at which you are standing yourself. Your theology should not work lazily with facile compromises. But a crystal clear thoroughly worked-out systematic theology would be based on a false system. In theology too you are pilgrims who seek the eternal homeland of truth in a constantly new exodus.

The Order's Potential for Change

There is yet another point of view from which I must discuss myself and my plan for the future influence of the Order. Seen in its historical perspective, the Society of Jesus today is usually considered as an Order of schools, theological learning, the book trade and higher Church management, and recently an Order of influence in the mass media. This is all well and good and indeed reflects the image that the Order has gained in its 400 years of history.

I have already said that the story of the sons is naturally, and quite properly, not merely the recapitulation of their forefathers' life. I have already said that I will not pass judgment on the past of the Order. This being so, I nonetheless ask, for your sake and for the sake of your future: What has this story actually to do with me and my way of life, especially from my 'primitive church' (as I used to call it) in Manresa onwards up until the first years after I finally settled in Rome, before work on the draft of the Order's constitution, the management of the Order and my illness absorbed me entirely?

We, my first companions and I, were not learned men, nor did we wish to be, even though it would have been easy enough for Francis Xavier, and Laínez was a needle-sharp theologian, who had made an impression on the Council of Trent. Of course, if you want to serve God and mankind with radical freedom of the spirit and without reservation, not tied down to anything and ready for everything, you must if need be, if you can and if the situation demands it, pursue high theology, write books, perhaps even become a court confessor in God's name, write letters to princes and prelates and people like them and so leave a mark for centuries on the history of the Order. But in my own decisive years we were, in fact, different from how we were to be portrayed in the later history of the Order.

We were really as poor as beggars and willingly so; we found shelter on our journeys through France and Italy in the filthy poorhouses of the time. We cared for invalids in hospitals (in Venice, for example, we cared for incurable syphilitics in two hospitals), and it was totally different from what is required of hospital staff today. We gave sermons in the streets, if need be in a gibberish of Spanish, Italian and French. We were proper beggars, catechism instruction for tiny children covered in lice was true faith in practice and not just a pious reminiscence, as it is in the modern formula of the vow for those joining the Order.

I myself took the initiative in founding the Gregoriana and the Germanicum, but I also founded the Martha House as a refuge for prostitutes in Rome. During the famine in Rome in 1538–9 we organized a vast feeding of the poor, when the streets of the Holy City were full of the dying, and starving children wandered around. I did not try to shut the girls up in a cloister as was the practice in those days, but did my best to bring them up for a life in the world worthy of a human being and for marriage. I encouraged the establishment of a home for girls in danger and supported orphanages. I founded a house for Jews and Moors who wanted to become Catholics. I did not regard it as too 'worldly' to bring about peace between Tivoli and Castell Madama. So even in my old age I was still active socially and politically. In my Basque homeland in 1535, during my last stay there, I took lodgings in the poorhouse at Azpeitia and ate with the poor what I had begged. I planned a well thought out scheme for the poor in my native town and put it into practice. I also founded schools and provided legally for their foundation and in addition modified the law of poverty of my Order a little, with a sigh, so that in many countries and centuries this Order has become an Order of schools and schoolmasters. I have truly nothing against this, if only the character and the whole mentality of the Order is not distorted by it. But do not forget that in my time these schools were run without payment of fees and so had a predominantly socio-political character, whereas today your schools *must* be expensive for the pupils, as I am the first to admit. There is much more that could be said on this subject.

I only wanted to ask one thing: Has the Order since then not neglected this side of my life? If so, perhaps historical necessity is the cause and I have already said several times that I do not lay claim to the history of this Order simply for myself alone. But must it remain so?

Is it possible for something to come alive once again in the future of this Order, something that I was truly concerned with in my discipleship of the poor and humble Jesus during my own life? Can the challenge that a new situation presents to the Order perhaps turn it in a new direction so that it remains true to its origins? In your 32nd General Congregation in 1974 you proclaimed anew 'the struggle for faith and justice' as the Order's task and acknowledged 'with repentance your own failure in the service of truth and in the commitment to justice'. You have understood the commitment to justice in the world as a profound and essential motive in your mission, far more than a mere optional addition to your proclamation of the gospel. You spoke of a 'complete and integral liberation of man' which leads to participation in the life of God himself'. I hope that you take your own words seriously. Your historical and social situation today is of course very different from mine in the sixteenth century, when purposeful planned changes in society could not be part of the task and duty of a Christian's love of his neighbour, as they are now. But I think, however, that if you take seriously the decisions of the 32nd General congregation, your highest court of decision, you will set out by a new road into the future on your one invariable mission. It is a road on which the man you call your father can accompany you in spirit.

How such a fight for greater justice in the world of the future will look exactly, I cannot prophesy. At all events you must not become politicians, nor party hacks, nor secretaries of large socio-political organizations, nor yet merely theoreticians of the so-called Christian social sciences. You must truly not seek for social power and not claim that you can serve your neighbour all the better the more power you have. That may be a secret maxim of actual politicians who seek to justify their profession, partly deceiving themselves, partly with complete honesty. It cannot be your maxim, neither in secular society nor in the Church, not even if you could really attain such power.

If you practise the discipleship of the poor and humble Jesus, if you accept that in the future your life in society may move onto the fringe far more than hitherto and if you accept this not under bitter duress but voluntarily in a position where you can truly carry out your fight for justice (you cannot imagine nowadays how the attitude of an outsider in terms of ecclesiastical society was implied by the refusal of my companions and myself to adopt the dress of an Order and other such symbols of ecclesiastical and social status), even if until your time very little came of that initial refusal in practical terms. As Melchior Cano quite rightly remarked, the fringe existence thus in evidence was felt to be quite incompatible with the ecclesiastically authorized life of an Order. The official Church today feels itself in much the same position *vis-à-vis* worker priests. So today you can still pursue learned theology, develop cultural and political strategies, deal in Church politics a little, broadcast on the mass media and so on. You may do all this as well. But you must not judge your life and the importance of the Order by your successes in these fields.

If it is only with sadness and resignation that you realize that this Order will never win back and no longer has the political, cultural and ecclesiastical importance that it possessed before its suppression in 1773, if this simple fact, which cannot be concealed, fills you with sadness and secret resignation, then you have completely failed to grasp what you ought to be. You should be men who seek to forget themselves for God's sake, who are disciples of the poor and humble Jesus, who preach his gospel, who stand by the poor and homeless in the fight for more justice for them. Can you no longer do this now and in the future? Does your work depend on all the power and glamour that the Society of Jesus once had or does such power fundamentally run the terrible danger of losing God because of trying to live without the death of Jesus?

For you there should and can be nothing in the world and in history, within and without, in heaven and on earth, that you can unreservedly and unconditionally love and strive for, except the mystery of God which you can trust unconditionally. Your Order which you love and its future, too, belong to the things that you accept calmly when they are sent to you and that you let go with equal calm when they are taken from you. I myself said in my own time that if the Order should collapse, I would not need more than ten minutes to be near to God and at peace again.

Prospects for the Future

To end I should like to say something about those who are not Jesuits. During my lifetime I had very faithful friends and companions in my Order, but also throughout my life many friends who were not Jesuits: high and low, rich and poor, learned and simple, good friends from other Orders, both men and women. I never imagined that they should all become Jesuits. For quite a few of them to whom I gave individual Exercises, the result was a radical conversion and awakening. They did not therefore become Jesuits, even where external circumstances would have made this possible and it would have been far easier than, for instance, in the case of a viceroy like Franz Borja. This is, of course, a foregone conclusion, but it is as well to put it into words.

Every way of life, and especially one that aims to mould a man right from his innermost self, presents a claim to universality, whether it wants to or not, a claim to general validity. It all too easily sees in other Christian ways of life, compared with its own, tentativeness and compromise, a lagging behind the radical maxims of life, which at best can merely be tolerated in silence as evidence of human inadequacy.

You have yourselves often practised such an understandable and foolish over-estimation of your own life-style during the course of your history. It is this which has given rise to the frequently heard and understandable accusation that the Jesuits are arrogant. But when and where such an exaggerated opinion of your own life-style and such a claim to universality is no longer possible even for the naive, because of the actual historical situation, the opposite danger arises. You become unsure of your own life-style and you are no longer certain that your own way of life is unconditionally valid for yourself, even if it is not suitable for everyone. So you seek a 'synthesis' of everything and everyone and produce nothing but a characterless mishmash that claims to be for tomorrow merely because it has mixed up together everything from yesterday. The man, however, who has won through to God's eternal freedom no longer needs to claim as his own everything that there is, in order to secure his own position. If one is in modest but certain possession of one's own position, one does not need to be excessively anxious to follow every fashion. Man's own future must grow from his own situation.

I have strayed from my theme into warnings. What I wanted to say is this: Today less than ever before does the world need to consist of people who are Jesuits or who are judged according to whether they are near you or far from you. Yet fundamentally you have a mission to these people who are not Jesuits and who do not want to be simply a smaller edition of the Jesuits either. Fundamentally, I say. For how far you will succeed with them, is not something that can be calculated in advance. It is a question not of calculation, but of hope and it is in the hands of the mysterious God of history.

But fundamentally you have a mission which can be addressed to all Christians and all men, even if what is of significance for everyone shows itself in an historically conditioned form and so in fact does not necessarily reach everyone. Providing this is borne in mind, what I lived and said and tried to show in my own life and that of my companions is still of general importance.

I can be counted, of course, among those people who stand at the gateway to the 'new era' in Europe. In spite of medieval characteristics in my life and work, what is new and individual in me is typical of the modern era, which is now approaching its end, even if no one can say what will come after it. It could be said that my 'spirituality' is typically modern, as much in its mystical individualism as in its rational and psychological technique and it also is nearly at an end. It could be said that ultimately this modernity of individualistic subjectivity and rationality alters nothing, that it would all remain embroiled in the vast machine of the Roman Church and be made use of by it, a machine which because of its age has even less chance in the future. But it is not so simple, at least not in the history of Christianity and the Church or in the case of historical phenomena which have occurred during the history of this Church and whose beginning does not simply mean the prognosis of the end. But let us give the history of theology a rest. In the Church things do not simply decline and fall because they had their origins in a definite era of Church history.

Perhaps my religious individualism, which has been described by you as 'modern', begins to take on new meaning when the individual is threatened with decline and extinction in an organized mass in the 'post-modern' era. I have nothing against it, Heaven forbid, if you seek to discover today in the religious sphere as earlier in the humanistic, a communal feeling, a living group, a basic fraternal community and feel yourself at home there. But be wary and sensible. The individual can never lose himself fully in the community.

Solitariness before God, security in his silent immediate presence is man's sole possession. And if this has become clearer at the beginning of the modern era in the Church, it is because it is a part of history which is not on the decline, but which remains and which should remain with your help too.

Will there one day, however, be men who fundamentally, through every phase of their existence, have no ear any longer for the word 'God'? Will there at some future date be men who no longer enquire after what is inexpressible in its endless variety? Will there one day be men who invariably and successfully reject the nearness of the mystery which namelessly rules their existence, which is one and all-embracing, the final cause and final goal? Does this mean that we drop into God's abyss lovingly addressing him as 'Thou' and can thus become free? What if this were possible, if this were real . . . ?

If it were so, it would leave me unmoved. Men would have evolved backwards, as individuals or as the whole human race, into resourceful animals and mankind's history of freedom. Responsibility, guilt and forgiveness would then be at an end – and only the manner of the end would have altered, for we Christians await an end in any case. Men who deserve the name of men would have found eternal life.

We can speak of God in future if we really understand what is meant by this word. There will always be a mysticism and mystagogy of the inexpressible nearness of God, who created another being in order to give himself in love as the gift of eternal life. Men can always be taught to demolish the finite images of idols which obstruct their paths or to pass them by calmly; can be taught not to make anything absolute; to become 'equable' and 'calm' in the face of all sorts of powers and forces, ideologies, goals and futures. In this way they learn what God is and that their freedom is not as empty as it seems.

There will always be men who on seeing the Crucified and Risen Jesus, pass by all the idols of this world and dare to give themselves unconditionally to the incomprehensibility of God, seen as love and mercy. How many they are numerically and in proportion to mankind as a whole is ultimately of no importance, if the Church alone as the sacrament of salvation for the whole world remains present in it. There will always be men who will stand by the Church in this faith in God and Jesus Christ, who will form it, carry it and even endure it, an historically tangible, institutional entity, which is at its most real (and so hardest and bitterest) for me in the Roman Catholic Church.

If there are always such men then I will always (however arrogant it may sound) have a mission for all men. For I only wanted to help man to understand this and to grasp my meaning. I did not ultimately want any special programme nor even any special way of being a Christian nor a special spirituality. Naturally I know that every man can inevitably, only pass on what is universally valid in his own way and so does not reach everyone. He may even, as it were, extinguish his own individuality, if he dares to preach about the eternal God and his Christ. So ultimately the question of a future history of the influence of my life and my teaching is irrelevant. Silent disappearance might be the greater act, since God remains ever the greater. May His Name be blessed.

Amongst much that has been said, much has remained unsaid and forgotten that you would have liked to hear from me. But I no longer even want to mention the subjects I might have chosen in preference to the ones discussed here. The end would be the same: a silence in which God's eternal praise is sung.

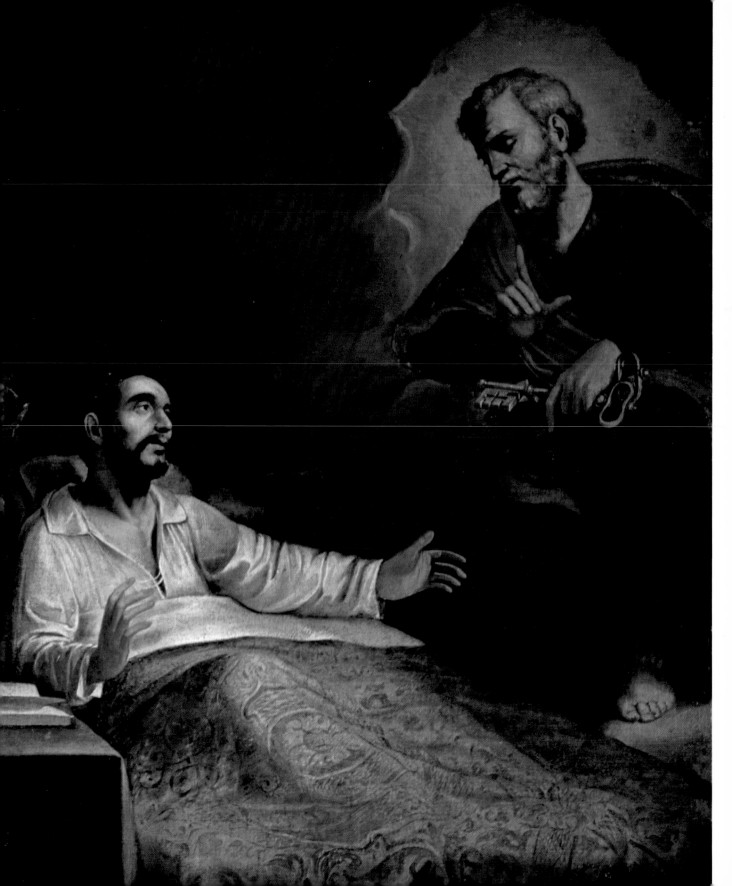

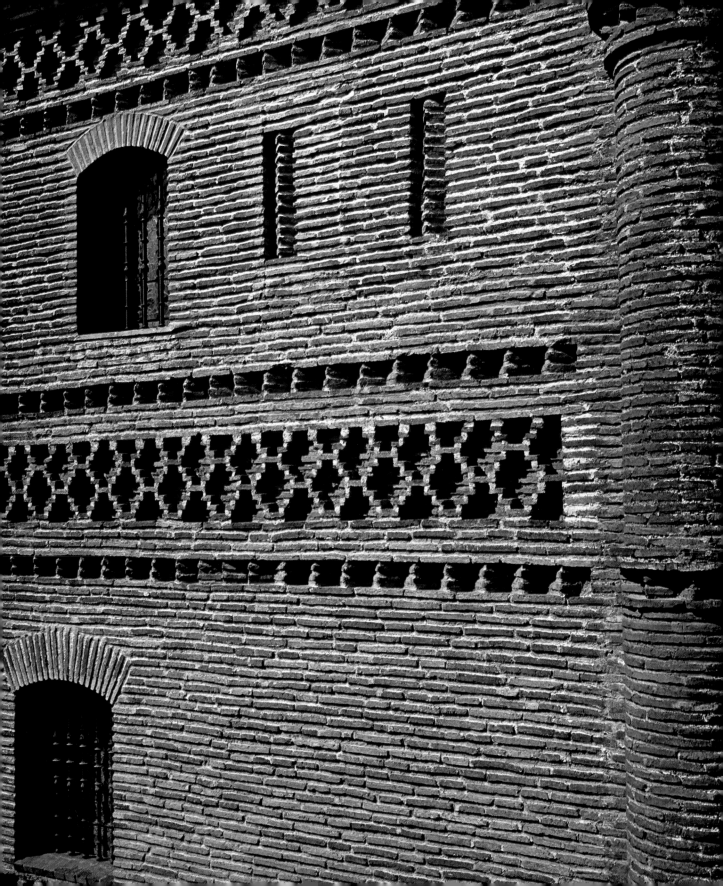

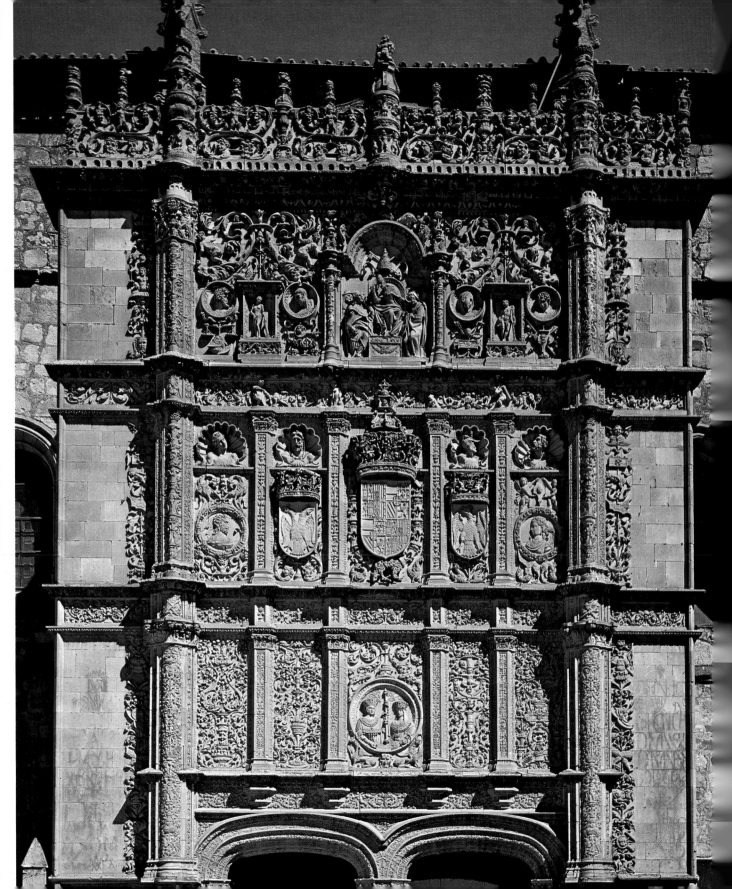

CVM SOCIIS FERVENTI= OR ARDET

S.IGNATIVS
PARISIIS IN MONTE MARTYRVM
FESTO ASSVMPTIONIS B.V.MARIÆ
CVM IX SOCIIS PER PRIMA VOTA

Picture Index

1 A relief on the facade of the doorway of the University of Salamanca, depicting Ferdinand of Aragon (1452–1516) and his wife, Isabella of Castile (1451–1504), the joint rulers of the two kingdoms that became the basis of modern Spain.

4 The fifteenth-century castle of Arévalo —a longtime residence of the young Queen Isabella—was the home of the royal grand treasurer, Juan Velázquez de Cuéllar, whom Ignatius served as a page and courtier from 1507–17.

2 The arms of the López de Loyola family, over the entrance to Ignatius of Loyola's birthplace. The López line can be traced back to the twelfth century, and their arms, one of the oldest among the Basque people, date from the beginning of the fourteenth century and depict a black kettle hanging on a chain between two rampant wolves.

5 The inner courtyard of the Collegio de San Gregorio in Valladolid, which was built by Enrique de Egas during 1488–96. It was here that Ignatius, as a member of the entourage of Antonio de Manrique, Duke of Nájera, took part in the reception of the Castilian Cortes (parliament), which in February 1517 pledged its allegiance to the young King Charles of Aragon (1500–58) (later Emperor Charles V 1519–58).

3 A late gothic baptismal chapel in the church of San Sebastián de Soreasu in Azpeitia. Ignatius, who was his parents' thirteenth child, was christened here in 1491 with the name of Iñigo López. On the top of the font there is a statue of Ignatius with the inscription 'Here was I baptized' written in Basque.

6 The city walls of Pamplona, principal city of the Basque Kingdom of Navarre, which was conquered by Spain in 1515. In May 1521 a French army, led by André de Foix, marched against Pamplona, capturing it on the 20th. It was during the defence of the city that Ignatius was seriously wounded in the leg by a cannon-ball.

7 The injured Ignatius being carried away from the battlefield by the victorious French. From a fresco, painted by Pozzo during 1685–92, which is in the choir of S Ignazio in Rome.

8 The Apostle Peter appears to Ignatius during the night before the Feast of Peter and Paul in 1521. It was from that night that Ignatius, who lay in his parents' house at Loyola near to death, began to recover. A painting by Carducho(?) finished, about the time of Ignatius's beatification, which is in the private chapel of Cardinal Odoardo Farnese in the new professional house of the Jesuits, near the church of Il Gesù in Rome. The foundation stone for this house was laid by the Cardinal in 1599, the work being completed in 1623 under the architect Girolamo Rainaldi.

9 Brickwork of the wall of the Loyola mansion. The foundations of the building were of square-hewn stones dating from the end of the fourteenth century and the rest of the building dates from 1461.

10 Mary appears to Ignatius during his convalescence in Loyola. A fresco painted in the second half of the seventeenth century by Jacques Courtois, called Borgognone, in the corridor outside Ignatius's rooms in the old professional house near Il Gesù in Rome.

11 Ignatius bids farewell to his brother before setting out on the journey to Montserrat. This fresco by Pozzo, dating from the end of the seventeenth century, is also in the corridor outside Ignatius's rooms, which are the only surviving part of the old professional house of the Order, which was incorporated into the new professional house (see no. 8). The corridor, with its baroque figures is decorated with frescoes, which not only depict scenes from Ignatius's life, but also the miracles of the saints.

12 The Madonna of Aranzazu is a thirteenth-century stone sculpture perched on the trunk of a thorn-tree. It was before this Madonna that Ignatius prayed for new strength for his journey to Montserrat.

13 Another of the frescoes in the corridor outside Ignatius's room by Pozzo. This one depicts the saint on his way to Montserrat.

14 The sandstone towers of Montserrat, high above the Catalan plain. On the east slope of this rocky bastion is a Benedictine abbey, founded in 1030, in whose church is kept the celebrated figure of the 'Black Madonna' (see below).

15 The 'Black Madonna' of Montserrat, a romanesquely-decorated wooden figure, dating from the end of the eleventh century. It was before this figure that Ignatius prayed during the night of 24 March 1522. On his departure he left his weapons as an offering.

16 This fresco by Pozzo shows Ignatius giving his rich clothes to a beggar at Montserrat.

17 A stone bridge over the Llobregat near Vilumara, over which Ignatius passed on his way to Manresa.

18 In Manresa Ignatius undertook a strict penance of fasting and flagellation. Fresco by Pozzo.

19 One of the caves near the River Cardoner near Manresa. It was here, in September 1522, that Ignatius experienced what he called his mystical 'primitive church'.

20 A fresco by Pozzo of Ignatius's great mystical experience of God at the Cordoner cave.

21 Ignatius begins to record his 'Spiritual Exercises' in Manresa. A section from a painting by Jusepe de Ribera (?), which was finished at the time of the beatification and hangs in the General's Court of the Society of Jesus in Rome.

22 The *Via Appia* near Rome. Ignatius travelled along this road before he arrived in Rome on 29 March 1523. Two days after his arrival in Rome, Ignatius received permission from Pope Hadrian VI to continue his pilgrimage to the Holy Land.

23 The clock tower, built by Coducci in 1496, on the north side of the Piazza San Marco in Venice. After his arrival in the city in May 1523, Ignatius attempted to obtain a passage on board a ship bound for Palestine.

24 The Venetian Senator Marcantonio Trevisano meets the exhausted pilgrim in the arched hall of the market place. It was through the Senator's mediation, and the help of other friends, that Ignatius obtained from the Doge, Andrea Gritti, free passage on board a Venetian pilgrim ship, which set sail for Palestine on 14 July 1523. A painting, either from the school of Rubens (?), or by Honthorst from the time of the beatification, in the private chapel of Cardinal Farnese in the new professional house in Rome.

25 A view from the Mount of Olives looking towards Jerusalem, with the Golden Gate in the city walls. Ignatius reached the city on 4 September 1523.

26 Detail from the wax model of Ignatius's head, taken from his death mask. The General's Court of the Society of Jesus in Rome.

27 The Great Hall of the University of Alcalá de Henares, where Ignatius studied from March 1526, after two years preparation in Barcelona.

28 Main gateway of the University of Salamanca, Ignatius entered the university on 10 July 1527 with the intention of setting down the religious pursuit of the 'Spiritual Exercises' and the Order's rules for life.

29 A view over the River Seine towards the Cathedral of Notre-Dame in Paris. In order to complete his studies, Ignatius travelled to Paris in February 1528. In March 1535 he received the official scroll of a Master of the Faculty of Arts of Paris.

30 On 15 August 1534, in the Chapel of the Martyrs in Montmartre, Ignatius and six companions took vows of poverty, chastity, the care of souls and a pilgrimage to the Holy Land. Pierre Favre (Peter Faber), the only priest among them, held a mass, during which the vows were made. A seventeenth-century glass window in the corridor outside Ignatius's rooms.

31 An altar in the castle chapel of Loyola. Above is a late gothic vesper painting and below, between saints Catherine of Siena and Catherine of Alexandria, is a Flemish painting of the Annunciation, which originally belonged to Queen Isabella, and then came into the possession of the Guevara family, relatives of the López of Loyola. In April 1535 Ignatius returned to his homeland from Paris and worked as a missionary among his fellow Basques.

32 A view from the old royal city of Toledo over the River Tagus. Here, in August 1535, Ignatius visited the parents of his companion Alphonso Salmerón, before setting sail from Valencia and leaving Spain for ever.

33 The facade of the church of SS Giovanni e Paolo in Venice, which stands alongside the so-called Hospital of Incurables. In January 1537 Ignatius and his companions worked in the hospital while they waited for the departure of the pilgrim ship.

34 A detail from a portrait of Ignatius attributed to Jacopino del Conte, one of his penitents. The painting was completed after Ignatius's death in 1556, for during his lifetime he always refused to be painted. The General's Court of the Society of Jesus, Rome.

35 A view which looks towards the cupola of St Peter's in Rome at dusk. Ignatius and his companions, Pierre Favre and Diego Laínez, returned to Rome in October 1537, after they realized that their pilgrimage to the Holy Land was jeopardized by the war between Venice and the Turks.

36 Just before he reached Rome, while praying at the chapel of La Storta, Ignatius had a vision of the Holy Trinity and heard from the Father the words, 'I wish to be merciful in Rome'. Ignatius also heard the Father say to Christ, 'I wish that you take this one as your servant'. This painting of the vision is from the school of the Caracci (Domenichino?) of 1609. The private chapel of Cardinal Farnese, Rome.

37 Ignatius writing the rules of his Order. Painting by Jusepe de Ribera (?) from the time of the beatification. The General's Court of the Society of Jesus, Rome.

38 Ignatius presents the rules of his Order to Pope Paul III. A seventeenth-century painting in the porch of the sacristy of the church of Il Gesù in Rome.

39 The image of the fourteenth-century 'Madonna della Strada' in a chapel near the burial altar of Ignatius in the church of Il Gesù. From February 1541 the Order lived in a house near the church of Santa Maria degli Astalli to which this image belongs. Ignatius had three small rooms in the old professional house which was built on this site in 1544.

40 Ignatius's seal and its impression. Whilst the seals of the later Generals of the Order under the sign IHS had three nails from the Cross as symbols of obedience, poverty and chastity, Ignatius's seal carried two stars and a half moon, perhaps signifying his longing for the Holy Land. The General's Court of the Society of Jesus in Rome.

41 A detail from the great ceiling fresco (1685–94) by Andrea Pozzo in the church of S Ignazio in Rome. Appropriate to the theme of the fresco—'Go and give light to the world'—are the symbolic figures in the corners of the painting of the four corners of the earth. This detail is of Asia.

42 A detail of the fresco showing Europe.

43 A detail showing America.

44 A detail showing Africa.

45 Francis Xavier is sent by Ignatius on a missionary journey to India in 1540. A seventeenth-century painting in the style of Pozzo, which hangs in Ignatius's room in Rome.

46 Ignatius's work-room with a door leading to a small balcony. Following the rules of the Order, Ignatius's rooms served as both a living and working area. Despite the baroque additions, the sparseness of the small rooms enables one even today to sense something of the spirit of the first Jesuits.

47 This view of the sky of Rome at night can be seen from the balcony of Ignatius's room.

50 The cupola of the church of Il Gesù seen from the garden in the south-east. The church, the mother church of the Jesuit Order, was the work of the architects Vignola and Giacomo della Porta and was begun in 1568 and finished in 1584. It is a model of roman baroque and the pattern for many Jesuit churches.

48 The death of Ignatius on 31 July 1556. A Spanish painting (by Carducho?) from the time of the beatification which hangs in the private chapel of Cardinal Farnese.

51 The central part of the great fresco by Pozzo which is over the middle aisle of S Ignazio. The artist carried out the theme given to him—'Go and give light to the world'—in such a way that the light of the Father passed through the heart of the Cross-bearing Son and then to the enraptured Ignatius, kneeling on the clouds, and from him to the four corners of the earth (see above).

49 The gravestone and burial altar of Ignatius in the church of Il Gesù. The altar, whose columns flank a silver statue of the saint by the sculptor Pierre Le Gros (1697), was built 1695–1700.

52 Part of the silver statue of Ignatius in the basilica of Loyola. The statue, sculpted by Francisco de Vergara the Younger, points with its right hand to a book on which the letters *Ad maiorem Dei gloriam* represent the motto of the Jesuit Order.

Ignatius of Loyola (1491-1556) an Historical Introduction

The pictures which accompany this introduction to the life of Ignatius are taken from the life of the founder of the Jesuit Order, which appeared in 1609 on the occasion of his beatification, and which were engraved by the Rubens School in Brussels.

Title and frontispiece from the Life

Origins and Background (1491)

Iñigo López de Oñaz y Loyola was born in 1491 in the Castle of Loyola near the small town of Azpeitia in the Basque province of Guipúzcoa. He came from one of the twenty-four families of the Basque nobility in Guipúzcoas. His family is first mentioned in documents dating from 1180 with the ancestor of his clan, Lope de Oñaz. In 1260 the grandson of his ancestor married the heiress Ines de Loyola.

Iñigo, who did not call himself Ignatius until he started studying in Paris, was the last child of Beltrán de Loyola and his wife Marina Saénz de Licona. He was baptised with the name of the saintly Benedictine abbot Eneco (in Basque Iñigo) of Oña who was revered in the Basque country. Iñigo grew up with his five sisters and seven brothers in a Catholic family which was proud of its martial and monarchist past.

When Iñigo came into the world, Spain was governed by the Catholic rulers, Ferdinand of Aragon and Isabella of Castile. During that period Cardinal Francisco Jiménez Cisneros was working towards the build-up of the kingdom as a new European power. In 1492 the last Moorish stronghold in Spain, Granada, had fallen, and in the same year Christopher Columbus, in the service of Queen Isabella, discovered America. It was a time of radical change, of discoveries and inventions. The Middle Ages were drawing to an end and a new era was beginning.

Secular Career (1506 - 21)

Iñigo was originally intended for the priesthood by his family. At a trial in 1515 – he was accused with his brother Pero López, the chaplain of Azpeitia – he attempted to escape the severity of the secular court by appealing to his tonsure in order to be brought before the less severe ecclesiastical court. However, for the most part, he preferred a 'worldly life'.

As the page of the royal treasurer, Juan Velázquez de Cuéllar, he received an education befitting his rank in Arévalo. He accompanied his master on journeys to the royal court and to Tordesillas. Iñigo led the life of a gallant and elegant courtier. He was often involved in duels, brawls and fights. When he was not furthering his ambitions for his career as a soldier, he was devoting himself to women and

1 Ignatius was severely wounded in the battle of Pamplona.

2 Saint Peter appears to the wounded Ignatius in Loyola.

3 During his illness Ignatius was stimulated by reading the life of Jesus and biographies of the Saints.

4 *Ignatius, whilst convalescing, experiences a vision of Mary.*

5 *Ignatius bids farewell to his brother.*

6 *On his way to Montserrat, Ignatius meets a Moor, with whom he has an argument.*

gambling; he admired in particular the Infanta Catarina, the youngest sister of the Emperor Charles.

After Velázquez's death in 1517, Iñigo found a new master in Antonio de Manrique de Laras, Duke of Nájera, Viceroy of Navarre. For him he defended Pamplona, the capital of Navarre, in 1521 with a few hundred men against an army of 12,000 under the command of the Lord of Esparros, André de Foix. Iñigo refused to surrender the city to the French without a fight and on 20 May he was severely wounded when a cannon ball shattered his right leg below the knee. The other leg too was badly damaged. After he had been injured the defenders of the citadel of Pamplona surrendered. The victorious French saw that Iñigo had medical attention and two weeks later he was carried on a painful fourteen day march through the mountains to his home at the castle of Loyola.

A Fresh Start in Loyola (1521 - 22)

After his return to Loyola it was discovered that the bones of Iñigo's right leg had been wrongly set. The leg was foreshortened and a bone protruded. On Iñigo's instructions a further operation was carried out which caused him great suffering. During the long and weary, as well as painful, healing process Iñigo was often at the point of death. During these months of convalescence time hung heavily on his hands. So he asked for exciting romances about cavaliers which were then fashionable reading. But as there were no such books in the castle he was forced instead to pass the time by reading the *Life of Christ* (*Vita Christi cartuxano*) written by the Carthusian, Ludolph von Sachsen, which had been translated into Spanish and given a preface by the Franciscan, Fray Ambrosio de Montesino. He also came across some lives of the saints (*Flos Sanctorum*) written by the Dominican Bishop, Jacobus de Voragine, with an introduction by the Cistercian, Fray Gauberto Maria Vagad.

During the time that Iñigo was ill he made a significant discovery in connection with these books. Whenever he thought about his past or future at court he took great pleasure in his reflections. But when the flood of thoughts and images was over he felt dissatisfied and out of humour. His fantasies about glorious military deeds of heroism and his plans for adventure left him flat and restless. When, on the other hand, he imagined emulating the saints and their deeds, he sensed the exhilaration of his mood afterwards. He was overcome with enthusiasm for St Francis and St Dominic. In his own psyche he experienced the first movements of Ignatian spirituality, the 'discrimination of the spirit'. 'Desolation' and 'consolation' as criteria for establishing God's will had become realities for him. In the course of his life he built on this basic experience in order to be able to lead others more effectively to the 'Spiritual Exercises'. He gathered together sets of rules to help men on the right track so that with God's grace they could find out how to live a life worthy of a human being.

In Loyola it seemed to Iñigo that his service to the greater honour of God consisted above all in doing penance. So he considered whether he should ask for acceptance in the Carthusian monastery of Seville or perhaps wander through the world as an unknown pilgrim, poor and despised. Even a pilgrimage to Jerusalem which he undertook around this time was planned as a penitential journey.

By the end of February 1522, Iñigo was sufficiently cured to leave his paternal castle. He wanted to begin a new life after his initial inner conversion.

Montserrat and Manresa (1522)

Accompanied by his brother Pero López, Iñigo made his way to Aránzazu, a place of pilgrimage cared for by the Franciscans, in order to pray. In Oñate he took leave of his brother to ride on to Navarrete. There he was given the pay still due to him by the Duke of Nájera, settled his debts and ordered a picture of Our Lady to be restored with the rest of the money. In March 1522 he set off for Catalonia and the famous mountain monastery of Montserrat. On the way there, in Pedrola, he was tempted to reach for his dagger during a heated theological argument with a Moorish travelling companion. In Ignalada, at the foot of Montserrat, he provided himself with beggar's clothing, such as pilgrims usually wore. He arrived at the gates of the monastery on 21 March 1522. He bequeathed his mule to the monastery and gave away his elegant clothes while his dagger and sword became his gifts to the Black Madonna of Montserrat. After three days' preparation Iñigo made a general confession to the pilgrims' father confessor, the Benedictine Juan Chanones. The night before the feast of the Annunciation, 25 March 1522, he spent with the other pilgrims at the feet of the Madonna.

The morning after his vigil in Montserrat, Iñigo left the world of the monastery and went to Manresa, which was about five hours' journey away. There he went to the Santa Lucia hospital for the poor; later he lived in a cell at the nearby Dominican monastery. For several months he stayed in Manresa as a ragged and ridiculed beggar. While living this mendicant life he suffered attacks of pro-

7 *Ignatius gives his clothes to a beggar.*

8 *Ignatius offers his sword to the Madonna of Montserrat.*

9 *In Manresa Ignatius is tormented by appearances of the devil as he prays.*

10 Ignatius sees the form of Christ in the Host during mass at Manresa.

11 The revelation to Ignatius in a cave near the River Cardoner.

12 In Manresa Ignatius begins to write down his 'Spiritual Exercises'.

found depression and inner despair. Disgust at his way of life and thoughts of suicide beset the penitent pilgrim. At this time too, however, he also had deep spiritual experiences about the mysteries of faith, the Trinity, the Creation and the humanity of Christ.

Iñigo changed his life-style after he had a visionary experience in a cave on the banks of the Cardoner which flows very near Manresa. Not only did he see everything differently again, but he also gained a new and profound awareness of the coherence and continuity of spiritual life, faith and theology.

Everything he had ever learnt in his whole life seemed insignificant in comparison. He felt he had become a new and changed man and that he had been given a new intellect. This was the source of his later striving through prayer to seek and find God in all things. He saw Jesus Christ from now on as the gentle king and lord who came to fulfil the spread of the kingdom of God which had dawned. Iñigo sensed his vocation to become a worker with and for Christ. The essential basic insights of his mystical experience by the Cardoner he put down in writing in his book of 'Spiritual Exercises'. This is how, for instance, his reflections on the king and the two army banners arose. Ignatius worked on the final form of this book of Exercises at a later time, during his periods in Paris and Rome.

Pilgrimage to Jerusalem (1523)

After staying in Manresa for about a year and a half, Iñigo started out on his longed-for pilgrimage to the Holy Land. On 18 February 1523 he left Manresa to go first to Barcelona. About four weeks later his ship sailed to the port at Gaeta in Italy and from there Iñigo travelled northwards. In Fondi, the Countess Beatrice Appiani, wife of the ruler, Vespasian Colonna, allowed him to enter the town to beg. On 29 March, Palm Sunday, he arrived at the Via Appia in Rome. Pope Hadrian VI granted him permission for the pilgrimage to the Holy Land. In the middle of April 1523 Iñigo set out on foot for Venice from where the ships full of pilgrims sailed for Palestine. Through the good offices of the Doge, Andrea Gritti, he was given a free passage on the trading vessel, the *Negrona,* which set sail on 14 July. In Famagusta on the island of Cyprus the pilgrims disembarked to continue their journey from Las Salinas in a small galleon.

They reached the harbour of Jaffa on 24 August 1523, but they were not allowed to land until 1 September. With a detachment of Turkish soldiers and two Franciscans they arrived in Jerusalem on

4 September. With great excitement Iñigo visited the Holy Places, exhilarated at being able to see and touch the places his Lord and Saviour Jesus Christ had known. After a stay of only twenty days Iñigo had to leave the Holy Land once again, as the local ecclesiastical authority, the Franciscan guardian of the Sion Monastery, Angelo da Ferrara, would not grant an extension of his permit to stay.

On 3 October the journey back to the sea began. On 14 October 1523 the galleon arrived once again in Cyprus. Iñigo was given a free passage on a small ship that was sailing to Apulia in Italy. He travelled on foot through Italy, finally reaching Venice in the middle of January 1524. During his return journey from the Holy Land he became convinced that he should study for a period and to that end he decided to go to Barcelona.

13 Ignatius travels to the Holy Land.

Barcelona (1524 - 26)

From February 1524 onwards Iñigo was once again on his travels. He crossed the theatre of war in Lombardy, being taken prisoner first by the Spanish, then by the French, before he reached Genoa. From there he sailed to Barcelona where Hieronymus Ardévol gave him private lessons in the rudiments of Latin. From October 1525 Iñigo and other younger pupils were able to benefit from Ardévol's public teaching. Two women, Isabel Roser and Inés Pascual, provided him with board and lodging. To help him serve his fellow-men he was joined in Barcelona by three companions, Calisto de Sá, Juan de Artiaga and Lope de Cáceres. They were to leave Iñigo again, however, before his stay in Paris which began in 1528.

By March 1526 his knowledge of Latin was sufficient for him to attend philosophy lectures at the university in Alcalá.

14 On the Mount of Olives Ignatius prays before the footprints of Christ.

Confrontations in Alcalá and Salamanca (1526 - 27)

In Alcalá Iñigo first found lodgings in the poor-house of Santa Maria La Rica, and later on in the Antezana hospital. His companions from Barcelona lived with families in the town. During this time Jean de Reynalde joined their company. They all wore sack-like grey cowls, and as well as studying at the university they took care of the poor of the town, as they had in Barcelona. In addition they gave catechism classes and instruction in the 'Spiritual Exercises', that is, they helped their fellow-men to discover God's will so that they were able to lead a more Christian Life.

Six months later in November 1526, they came into contact with

15 Ignatius is brought back to the monastery by a watchman, because he had stayed too long on the Mount of Olives.

16 Ignatius gives his travel money to beggars.

17 Ignatius in the grammar school in Barcelona.

18 Ignatius preaches from prison.

the Inquisition for they were suspected of being *alumbrados* or illuminati, adherents of a quasi-quietist and elitist sect. After a decision by the Vicar General, Juan Rodrigues de Figueroa, on 21 November 1526, they had to have their grey cowls dyed a distinctive colour, so that they could be more easily recognized by their clothing, and so that it was clear that they were not part of an order in the strict ecclesiastical sense. Yet the suspicions and ecclesiastical admonitions did not cease even then. On 19 April 1527, Good Friday, Iñigo was ordered to spend 42 days in prison. During another trial in Alcalá, on 1 June 1527, new injunctions regarding their clothing were made against him and his companions. For Iñigo, however, the hardest part of the verdict was that he and his companions were prohibited from discussing matters of faith in Alcalá for the next four years, even though nothing heretical could be proved against their pastoral work. Before they could take up their spiritual activities again, they had to finish their remaining studies in accordance with the judgment given at the trial.

Iñigo and his companions preferred therefore to move to the Salamanca diocese, on the advice of the Archbishop of Toledo and Primate of Spain, Alonso de Fonseca y Acebedo, with whom Iñigo had stayed in Valladolid after his last trial. In the middle of July 1527 Iñigo arrived in Salamanca only to be imprisoned twelve days later for 22 days at the instance of the Dominican monastery of San Esteban on suspicion of heresy. His notes on the 'Spiritual Exercises' were examined carefully, although nothing heretical could be discovered in them. Nonetheless he was forbidden to speak any further on the difference between mortal and venial sin without first making a thorough study of moral theology.

In the middle of September 1527, Iñigo separated from his companions and left Salamanca in order to study in Paris. On the way he spent three months with friends in Barcelona. At the beginning of the year 1528 he started out on foot, reaching Paris on 2 February 1528.

Studies in Paris (1528 - 35)

Iñigo began his studies in Paris at the Montaigu College, one of the most famous centres of learning in Western Europe, which was renowned for the rigour of its academic studies and for the ascetic life of its members. He studied there as an external student from February 1528 to September 1529. Exactly two months after Iñigo's arrival in Paris he was once again without resources of any kind as an acquaintance had stolen most of the twenty-five ducats that Isabel Roser had given him before he left Barcelona. So he moved into the pilgrim hospice of St Jacques. He intended to finance his studies by begging but going out to beg daily wasted valuable time that he should have spent studying. So he undertook three begging journeys during the vacations between semesters. During Lent 1529 he went to Bruges where he found lodgings in the house of Gonzalo de Aguilera. In Antwerp he was helped by Juan de Cuéllar in particular, who also generously gave him money for the two other begging journeys in the summer of 1530 and 1531. His last begging journey which took him as far as London, was especially remunerative.

19 Ignatius is reinstated by the Rector of the University.

These begging journeys and regular remittances from benefactors not only made Iñigo's studies secure financially but even enabled him to help his fellow-students. After his first begging journey he gave the 'Spiritual Exercises' to three students, Juan de Castro, Pedro de Peralta and Amador de Elduayen, so that they could endeavour to follow a more resolute discipleship of Jesus. They gave their possessions to the poor and moved into the pilgrim hospice of St Jacques. This caused such an outcry among the Spanish colony in Paris that they were forced to give up their new way of life. So this attempt of Iñigo's to win companions ended in failure.

On 1 October 1529 Iñigo began a three and a half year philosophy course. He was now studying at the college of Sainte-Barbe of which Diego de Gouvea was director. With Master Juan de la Peña, Pierre Favre (Peter Faber) from Savoie and Francisco de Jassu y Xavier (Francis Xavier) from Navarre he moved into a small lodging in the college. At the end of the philosophy course he passed the Baccalauréat examination. It is in this connection that he is first listed in the University records as Ignatius of Loyola. A year later, on 13 March 1533, after additional examinations he gained his degree in philosophy and it is after this and his inaugural lecture in March 1535 with its solemn ceremony that he became known as Magister Ignatius. During these last two years of his stay in Paris he also studied scholastic theology in the Dominican monastery of Saint Jacques.

20 In Paris Ignatius wins new companions.

During his years studying philosophy Ignatius had won new friends, who wanted like him to lead a radically apostolic life according to the Gospel. On 15 August 1534, the feast of the Assumption, the circle of friends, Ignatius of Loyola, Nicolás Bobadilla, Pierre Favre, Diego Laínez, Simon Rodrigues, Alfonso Salmerón and Francisco de Xavier met in the Chapel of the Martyrs in Montmartre to take their vows. At the celebration of the Eucharist by the newly ordained

21 Ignatius also escapes a murder plot in Paris.

22 Ignatius and his companions make their vows in Montmartre.

23 Ignatius is enthusiastically received in Spain.

24 Ignatius preaches to the people of Spain.

priest, Pierre Favre, they made a promise before receiving communion of poverty, chastity and to make a pilgrimage to Jerusalem. If it proved impossible to carry out the pilgrimage and stay in the Holy Land, they proposed to put themselves at the disposal of the Pope as the Vicar of Christ, whom they considered as having the best overall view of the needs of Christendom. At this time in Paris they had no plans to establish their own Order.

At the beginning of April 1535 Ignatius, on the advice of doctors and his friends, agreed to look after his failing health by returning to his Basque homeland. Before he left he handed over the leadership of the circle of friends to Pierre Favre. They did not intend to meet again until the spring of 1537 in Venice and his companions intended to pursue their theological studies in Paris. Before the meeting in Venice they had been joined by Paschase Broët, Jean Codure and Claude Jay.

Travels in Spain (1535)

From Paris Ignatius rode through France for three weeks by way of Bayonne to Azpeitia, in the Basque country. In spite of his family's wishes he refused to live in his father's castle at Loyola, staying instead in the Santa Magdalena Hospital of the Poor in Azpeitia. He provided his living expenses by begging. He also gave penitential sermons and catechetical instruction and helped draw up a new plan for the poor in Azpeitia, which came into force on 23 May 1535. He helped too in the reform of the clergy of Azpeitia, two treaties relating to this being signed on 18 May and 23 June 1535. One month later he drew up the documents for his sister Magdalena's will.

Meanwhile Ignatius's health improved to such an extent that by the end of July 1535 he began his travels yet again. At Puerto de Echegárate he left his native province of Guipúzcoa. Passing through Pamplona he travelled via Obanos, Almazán, Toledo and Madrid to Valencia. On this journey he visited the relatives of some of his friends who were still in Paris. In Segorbe he was a guest of his friend Juan de Castro, the Carthusian, for eight days. About the end of October 1535 Ignatius sailed from Valencia to Genoa.

Venice (1535 - 37)

After a brief stay in Bologna, Ignatius arrived in Venice at the end of 1535. In the following year he several times gave 'Spiritual Exercises' and made contact with people in circles interested in

Church reform, such as Pietro Contarini, Gasparo de Dotti, Gian Pietro Carafa, the co-founder of the Theatine Order and Jaïme Cazador, who was later Bishop of Barcelona. However, most of his time in Venice was devoted to a thorough study of theology.

Ignatius's nine companions from Paris arrived in Venice after a winter journey lasting nearly two months on 8 January 1537. Since the pilgrim ships to the Holy Land only set sail in the middle of the year, they undertook the care of the poor and sick in the town in the meantime. Their main places of work were the hospital attached to the church of San Giovanni e Paolo and at the so-called Hospital of Incurables. In the middle of March 1537 all except Ignatius went to Rome to ask for permission for a pilgrimage to the Holy Land. The non-priests among them also requested leave to be ordained, although they were not members of an Order and had no bishop with jurisdiction over them. All their wishes were fulfilled and in addition a collection was made for them in the Papal Curia which amounted to 210 ducats. As soon as they were back in Venice they made a public vow of poverty and chastity together with Ignatius before the papal legate Girolamo Veralli. On 24 June 1537, the feast of St John the Baptist, they were ordained by Vincenzo Nigusanti, the Bishop of Arbe in Dalmatia.

Because of political tensions with the Turks there was no pilgrim ship to the Holy Land in the summer of 1537. But the companions counted on the political situation changing soon, so that they might still risk undertaking their pilgrimage. While they waited for the situation to change they split up into small groups in the nearby towns.

The Path to Rome (1537)

The group composed of Ignatius of Loyola, Pierre Favre and Diego Laínez left Venice on 25 July 1537 and found shelter in the half-ruined monastery building of San Pietro in Vivarolo outside the city walls of Vicenza, where they led a poor and frugal life. Forty days after their arrival Ignatius gave his first sermon in Italian. It was composed of a barely intelligible mixture of Spanish, French, Latin and Italian and began with the words '*Hojourdi* (today) *Sancta Mater Ecclesia*'. The pastoral work undertaken by Ignatius, Favre and Laínez in Vicenza lasted until the end of September, when Ignatius summoned his other companions to Vivarolo so that they could all consider their future together. The pilgrimage to the Holy Land was by now impossible, since Venice had been at war with Turkey since 13 September 1537. The companions all agreed to postpone the pilgrimage until the

25 Ignatius travels from Spain to Italy.

26 In Venice, with his companions, Ignatius becomes a priest.

27 In Rome Ignatius has a vision of God the Father and of Christ.

28 Ignatius celebrates his first mass in Rome.

29 Ignatius receives from Pope Paul III his approval of the Order.

30 Ignatius sends Francis Xavier to India as a missionary.

following year. If no opportunity offered itself then, the clause concerning the Pope in the Montmartre vow would come into force and they would consequently be guided by the Pope's plans in their work. It became clear to them during their discussions and prayers in Vivarolo that it was clearly God's will that they should spend the next few months doing pastoral work in the larger towns of Northern Italy.

During their days together in Vicenza they fastened on to the name the *Compañia de Jesus*, the Society of Jesus, as the most appropriate name for their covenant. They acknowledged that their sole head was Jesus Christ, whom alone they wanted to serve. In his discipleship they wanted to live radically for their fellow-men, by concerning themselves with others' problems and needs so that in this way too God's love for mankind would be made visible.

After the discussion was concluded, Ignatius set out in the direction of Rome with Favre and Laínez. As he travelled on the road from Sienna to Rome Ignatius felt in his heart that God was saying to him: 'I will show you favour in Rome'. He prayed to the Mother of God that her son would take him under his banner.

In November 1557, about ten kilometres north of Rome, at the last mile-post outside the town, Ignatius went into the little church of La Storta on the Via Cassia to pray. There he experienced a mystical enlightenment, similar to that he had known at Manresa, in which he was profoundly moved by a conversion of his heart and soul with the three-fold God. In this 'vision' at La Storta he saw how God the Father joined him to Christ his Son, so that he could no longer have any doubts at all. It was Christ poor, scorned, and carrying the Cross to whom he now knew that he and his companions were united. Ignatius heard Jesus saying: 'I want you to serve us.' For Ignatius this experience meant divine corroboration of his work up until now.

By the middle of November 1537 he had reached Rome, the Eternal City, which was to be his home until his death.

The Years in Rome (1537 - 56)

In Rome Ignatius and his two companions, Pierre Favre and Diego Laínez, were able to live for the time being in the country house of the nobleman Quirinio Garzoni at Pincio near the Church of Trinità dei Monti. In June 1538 they moved into a house near the Ponte Sisto, because their other companions had arrived in Rome at Easter 1538. Since his own arrival in Rome Ignatius had spent the time almost exclusively explaining the Exercises. He had even accompanied the Cardinal Gasparo Contarini in the 'Spiritual Exercises'.

Pope Paul III (1534–49) gave Ignatius and his circle of friends pastoral work to do in Rome. They preached, heard confessions and gave catechetical instruction. But Ignatius once more came under suspicion of heresy because of an argument about the true faith with the Augustinian hermit Agostino Mainardi. After a long struggle it was confirmed in the name of the Pope on 18 November 1538 that he and his companions were in complete harmony with the Church. Soon after the confirmation of their orthodoxy and loyalty to the Church they put themselves at the disposal of the Pope—who accepted their offer—for apostolic work in accordance with their vows at Montmartre. Since they had now given up their plans for a pilgrimage to the Holy Land, they sent back to their benefactors—to their considerable astonishment—the 210 ducats they had been given.

In the late autumn of 1538 they moved to the empty house of the Frangipani, near Torre del Melangolo. The winter of 1538–39 was unusually severe and long. Even in the countryside around Rome the reserves of food were exhausted; in the town itself famine broke out. Many people starved or froze to death. Ignatius and his companions gave shelter to hundreds of needy people on the Frangipani estate. In other areas of the town they looked after almost 3000 people altogether. In the midst of this time of suffering Ignatius celebrated his first holy Mass on Christmas Day 1538 in the church of Santa Maria Maggiore.

When on 19 March 1539 Pope Paul III sent Paschase Broët and Simon Rodrigues to Sienna, Ignatius and his friends started long discussions and prayers at the end of March 1539. They considered whether they should dissolve their community or whether they should stay together and found an Order. They weighed up the reasons for and against the possibilities. These debates, which lasted until 15 April 1539 resulted in the decision to take a vow of obedience to one of their number and to establish an Order. The name of the Order was already decided: *Compañía de Jesus*, the Society of Jesus. They saw no presumption in adopting this title; their intention was to express their desire for their community to grow more and more in the service of Christ for the Church. On 3 May 1539 the further results of their deliberations were gathered together in eleven chapters. Between then and 24 June 1539 many important questions were clarified. It was, for instance, decided that there should be no codified penitential exercises for the members of the Order. At the end of June 1539 Ignatius collected together in the *Prima Instituti Summa*, the first draft of the statutes of the Order called the Society of Jesus. The five chapters, of which the document consists, were carefully scrutinized by the Dominican Tom-

31 After his election as General of the Order, Ignatius and his companions lay down the vows of the Order.

32 Ignatius defends the innocent before the court.

33 In Rome Ignatius founded several Homes and Institutions.

34 *Ignatius receives from Pope Julius III approval for the establishment of the Collegium Romanum.*

35 *Ignatius often prayed under the stars.*

36 *Ignatius disturbed at prayer by his secretary.*

maso Badia on behalf of the Papal Curia and laid before Pope Paul III by Cardinal Gasparo Contarini in Tivoli on 3 September 1530, where they were given verbal approval by the Pope. Nevertheless, Ignatius had to fight for another whole year to secure the final written recognition of the new Order by the Pope. In the process he was involved in disagreements with Cardinal Girolamo Ghinucci and, more seriously, Cardinal Bartolomeo Guidiccioni, who was fundamentally opposed to the founding of any new Orders.

On 27 September 1540, however, Pope Paul III had the Bull *Regimini Militantis Ecclesiae*, the document establishing the Jesuit Order, drawn up. It approves the special characteristics of the Order, for instance, the name 'Society of Jesus', the universal apostolate and the vow of special obedience to the Pope. Through the papal document the Order also gained the right of electing a Superior General and setting out regulations for the Order, which was allowed to have sixty members.

At the beginning of 1541 the companions decided that Ignatius should work out proposals for the constitutions with Jean Codure, for example the rules about poverty over which Ignatius toiled with great patience and care during the following years, as is clear from his *Spiritual Journal*. From the 4th March 1541 all the members of the Order present in Rome worked on the text of the constitutions. It was agreed by all the members to choose a Superior General for life.

At the election of 2 April 1541 Ignatius was unanimously chosen; he alone wrote on his voting paper that he chose the one for whom most votes were cast, excepting himself. When a new election held on 13 April showed the same result, Ignatius withdrew to the monastery of San Pietro in Montorio. His father confessor there, the Franciscan Fra Teodosio da Lodi ordered him to accept his election and Ignatius consented. On the morning of 22 April 1541 he went with five companions to the church of San Paolo Fuori Le Mura to make a solemn vow of profession with them, the expression of the closest bond with the Order. The first Jesuits made their promises for life at the hands of the founder of their Order.

At the beginning of February 1541 the *Societas Jesu* (SJ), as it was called in Latin-speaking Rome, transferred to the church of Santa Maria degli Astalli, which contained the miraculous image of the Madonna della Strada. On 15 May 1542 Ignatius took over this church according to Canon Law in his capacity as Superior General of the Order. Beside the church a simple new house was built, where Ignatius lived from then on. From here he led the Order during his remaining years. Almost seven thousand letters and instructions have been preserved, many of them extremely detailed. In 1553, for instance, he writes a long letter on obedience to Simon Rodrigues, the Provincial of Portugal. Through such letters he was able to stay in constant touch with his fellow brothers who had scattered to work throughout the world. Francis Xavier, for instance, was in India and Japan from 1540 onwards. Although the new Order had to contend with many hostilities, especially at the hands of Melchior Cano in Spain, it increased steadily in membership and among those admitted to the Order was Francisco de Borja, the Duke of Gandia.

37 *Philippus Neri often recognized a nimbus around Ignatius during his lifetime.*

In spite of the numerous tasks involved in being head of the Order, Ignatius continued to give Exercises, wrote many spiritual letters, gave instruction in the catechism and preached sermons. In addition he established places of charity in Rome, like the Martha House for former prostitutes and next to the church of Santa Catarina dei Funari a home for girls who were in particular danger of exploitation. He provided for orphanages and concerned himself with the care of the poor. He had a house built near the Capitol for Moors and Jews who wanted to adopt the Christian faith. He made peace between hostile towns and reconciled families, and the Pope and many of the cardinals sought his advice.

After lifting the restriction on the number of members belonging to the Society with the Bull *Iniunctum nobis* on 14 March 1544, Pope Paul III agreed to the proposal of the Superior General on 5 June 1546 that not only priests but lay people from every walk of life could be accepted into the Order if they took the vows. This is a regulation which still applies today.

38 *The death of Ignatius.*

After it had been approved by the papal brief *Pastoralis officii* on 31 July 1548, Ignatius published a book containing the methods and details for the Exercises. He had already written down essential passages after his religious experiences in Loyola and Manresa. From them emerged a book the truth and power of which is scarcely evident to the casual reader, but which is fully revealed to the student of the Exercises. The book of *Spiritual Exercises* and the spirit which inspires it and those who use it have been the source of one of the greatest intellectual and spiritual movements in subsequent centuries.

In so far as he found time as Superior General, Ignatius worked constantly on the statutes of the Order, praying over many of the details until a clear decision could be made. From 1547 onwards he received excellent help in his work on the constitutions from his secretary Juan de Polanco. After Pope Julius III had solemnly ratified the Order in the brief *Exposcit debitum,* the members of the Order whom Ignatius had summoned to Rome at the turn of the

39 *Miraculous signs at the commitment of the bones of the saint in the church of Il Gesù in Rome.*

40 The canonization of Ignatius by Pope Gregory XV.

year 1550/51, deliberated on the prepared draft of the ten part constitution and the general examination containing the questions to be put to those wanting to join the Order. The draft was agreed unanimously. Ignatius continued working on details of the statutes almost until the day he died. The approval of the statutes on the side of the Order took place in 1558 through the first General Congregation of the Society of Jesus. On 30 January 1551 Ignatius asked his assembled brothers to transfer the guidance of the Order to someone else, but they refused. Ignatius yielded and worked on. On 22 February 1551 the 'Roman College', a Jesuit foundation, was opened. Here the academic basis for a reform of the Church was worked out. In a short time the foundation house was full up and the college moved into a new building near San Stefano del Cacco. Later the papal Gregorian University developed here in close connection with the college. In October 1552 there followed the founding by Ignatius of the Collegium Germanicum et Hungaricum, in which German priests and students of theology have been educated up to the present day.

At the repeated and insistent request of his brothers, especially Jerónimo Nadal, Ignatius began in the early spring of 1553 to dictate to his brother Luis Gonçalves da Câmara the story of his spiritual life in the years from 1521 to 1539. But only a first part of the dictated autobiography was completed. They did not begin work on it again until the autumn of 1555 when they completed the 'Account of the Pilgrim', the story of the divine guidance experienced by Ignatius.

By 1556 the Order had grown to a thousand members working in thirteen provinces. There were one hundred and ten houses for the Order, twenty of them in Italy. Many of the houses were colleges, forty-six of them in Europe alone. They were public schools which also served for the academic education of the Order's novices.

In his last years Ignatius suffered from a severe liver disorder. On the evening of 30 July 1556 he knew that he was about to die. His secretary Juan de Polanco did not want to send for the papal blessing for the dying until the next morning. Ignatius concurred with the words: 'Do as you will, I am totally in your hands'. One of the brothers in a neighbouring room heard him praying softly at midnight: 'O my God'. He died without the last sacraments in the early hours of the 31 July 1556 at the age of sixty-five. In the evening of 1 August 1556 his body was buried in the church of Santa Maria della Strada. It was transferred from there to the church of Il Gesù in 1587.

After his beatification in 1609 by Pope Paul V, Ignatius was canonized on 12 March 1622 by Pope Gregory XV.

Further Reading

St Ignatius Loyola: Spiritual Exercises, trans. by T. Corbishley; Anthony Clarke Books, Wheathampstead.

BIOGRAPHICAL STUDIES

Ignatius His Conclave, ed. T. S. Healey; O.U.P., Oxford.

St Ignatius Loyola: Autobiography, ed. John C. Olin, trans. by J. F. O'Callaghan; Torchbooks, Harper and Row, London and New York.

Ignatius Loyola and the Jesuits, by John Catling Allen; Hulton Educational Publications, Amersham.

Life of Blessed Father Ignatius of Loyola, by Pedro De Ribadeneira; Scolar Press, London.

GENERAL WORKS

The English Jesuits, by Bernard Basset SJ; Burns and Oates, London.

A History of the Society of Jesus, by William V. Bangert SJ; The Institute of Jesuit Sources, St Louis University, Missouri.

The Jesuits' Catechism, by Etienne Pasquier; Scolar Press, London.

The Jesuits: A History of the Society of Jesus, by Rene Fulop-Miller; Putnam, New York.